# Métis/Acadian Heritage 1604 to 2004

## Roland F. Surette
## Eastern Woodland Métis Nation
## Nova Scotia

**Cover Photo:**

The cover photo gives us a look at one of the many moose that used to be harvested in the Quinan (Mi'kmaq name Machoudiak) hunting community. This photo was taken in the 1930's. The Métis/Acadian hunter on the left is Leandre Frontain (1907- 1986) married a woman from Meteghen and moved *Par-en-Haut* (Up-the-Bay) where he made his living. Each fall, however, he returned to his traditional hunting grounds, often accompanied by his friend, to the right in the photo, Emile Deveau. People may remember Emile as their ESSO oil delivery man in Yarmouth in years gone by. The treat of winter meat and a backwoods experience had him park the oil truck and team up with Leandre whenever the opportunity presented itself. This photo was lent to me for this publication by Paul Tufts, a man well known and well respected in this part of the country as a woodsman with few equals. Paul's life's work has been a career in lands and forest management combined with fur trapping and wildlife management. As a young lad, growing up in Meteghen, Paul was taken *under the wing* by Leandre Frontain, learning to respect nature, learn its secrets, and try to leave it as good as you found it.

Leandre comes from a long line of Métis/Acadian woodsmen. Let me take you back six generations. Leandre Frontain; son of (1) Jean Baptiste (John) Frontain b. 10/01/1867 & Marie Anne (Mary) Mius (Robert & Julienne Mius); son of (2) Simon Frontain (called Mure Noire) b. 11/12/1837 & Jeanne Mius (Jean Baptiste & Marie Henriette Mius); son 0f (3) Marc Frontain b. 12/12/1808 & Anne Elisabeth Mius (Jean Baptiste a Laurent & Genevieve Moulaison); son of (4) Augustin (Justin called Buss) Frontain married 19/08/1807 Isabelle (Elizabeth) Doucet (Michel & Marie Mius); son of (5) Victor Frontain married Marguerite Corporon (Eustache); son of (6) Alexandre Julien Frontain married Anne d'Azy Mius b04/11/1736 (Francois d'Azy Mius). Leandre, like many who emanate out from the Quinan community, is steeped with Métis blood and culture. It is for this reason that you find him in front of this publication.

Published by:   Roland F. Surette
                P.O. Box 415
                116 Richard's Road
                Lower Wedgeport, Nova Scotia  B0W 2B0
                Phone: (902) 663-2817

Printed by:     Sentinel Printing Limited
                1-800-565-3043
                Yarmouth, N.S.  B5A 1S7

**Library and Archives Canada Cataloguing in Publication**

Surette, Roland F., 1951-

    Métis/Acadian heritage 1604 to 2004 / Roland F. Surette

Includes bibliographical references.

ISBN 0-9736116-0-X

    1. Métis--Nova Scotia--History. 2. Acadia. I. Title.

FC109.S87 2004          971.6'00497          C2004-904251-3

# Dedication

In 1972, I was taking a course from the late Professor W.S.McNutt, author of: The History of Atlantic Canada. The course that he was giving at Saint Thomas University was given the same name. This grand old gentleman was not one to try to remember all of the names of his students.

We were in excess of one hundred in the classroom. Me, however, he singled out as Messieur the Acadian in the back row. On several occasions, he informed me that I, as an Acadian, must know about the Cairn at Jemseg, situated along the banks of the Saint John River in New Brunswick. His point, of course, was what it symbolized for the early Acadians.     My hitherto education, in the English dominated curriculum vis-‡-vis. the history of Canada in the Nova Scotia school system, left me completely unawares of its significance. Let me assure you that I soon did find out the answer Professor McNutt sought and neither what happened at Fort Saint Marie nor my ignorance about my own family history has since been forgotten. I must thank an old man who thought that I should make time to know my own family history before trying to know about others.

Indirectly, he is one of the reasons that this effort has been made to set the record straight. To Professor W.S.McNutt, I dedicate the historical aspects of this book. I wish only that he were alive today to help me in the polishing of this document.

The two other people that I dedicate the efforts, of a once wayward son, are my parents: the late Edwin Frederick Surette and Josephine Jacqueline (Murphy) (Surette) Cotreau. This special couple made a scholar out of a man hell bent on becoming a fisherman. Of the many decisions that a young man has to make starting out in life, this was perhaps my greatest. Thank you for bringing our family to the many historical places in Atlantic Canada when we were kids. This whetted my appetite for knowledge, an appetite that has not waned after all these years.

I also must mention my grand daughters, Baylee Morgan, and Taylor Erynn Natalie, who, at the ages three and two respectively, are my "Sanity Clause". Nothing can make a person more upbeat than the unconditional love young people give to adults who make a difference in their lives.

Last, but not least, I thank Raymond Muise for his invaluable research, Carole Jacquard for her proof-reading skills, and Donald LeBlanc for his all-round assistance. Both suffering from long term illness, Donald and I are only half the men we used to be, but, put us together – what a man!

Lower Wedgeport, Nova Scotia                    Roland F. Surette

26 April2004

*This author attended a Métis Rights Forum in the Toronto Convention Centre 19-21 November2003. The forum was a direct result of the Supreme Court of Canada Decision, handed down 19 September2003, with regards to the Powley family right, as Métis, to hunt moose in the Sault Ste Marie community. This is as close as I got to an actual moose.*

*Replica of the type of ships used to ply the waters of the Atlantic for exploration and colonization. They had to be seaworthy yet not draw too much water to allow for coastal navigation.*

# Contents

*Ellen (Clairmont) Surette and daughter, Amber,*
*in the Grande Prairie region of Alberta.*
*People from her family tree headed west to form part of the*
*Métis people there.*

# Introduction

It is our contention that Métis/Acadian history has been fragmentary at best. In the earlier English-biased textbooks, students have been fed tidbits about "Acadie", stressing its early beginnings and often culminating with the ultimate British solution, THE DEPORTATION 1755-1763. Every author has his or her bias. Our bias is to give a fair shake to those early peoples of Acadia, both the First Nations and their mostly French friends. Lessons learned in the beginning were mutual respect, mutual appreciation, and mutual aid. The democratic ways absorbed by the latter group from the former, combined with a strong sense of family on both sides, helped create our Métis/Acadian ancestors.

Your identity is so much of who you are. It is a clarification of the ethnic/racial building blocks that make up a human being. You end up knowing who you are, how you got here, where you belong and how to celebrate the diverse ancestors who have given you life. If you can feel good within your own skin, it becomes contagious. Pass on this sense of well being to others, whether they share a similar history or merely wish to share our uniqueness with us.

Sharing within our community, with the Elders, other family members, neighbors, or others who are in need is very important to the Métis/Acadian culture. Successful hunters and other food gatherers give part of their bounty to others with an open heart. They realize that in order for a community to survive and thrive, all of its members must have access to the necessities of life. Also, on another given day with different circumstances, the giver may become the recipient. A strong sense of family and extended family gave birth to many of the small Métis/Acadian communities in Acadie. Families pulled together for the common good.

Clearing/dyking land, home/barn raising, weir/boat fishing, hunting/food gathering and the fur trade kept our ancestors busy. Marriages were often deferred to the early fall after the harvest or prior to the hunt. Children were often celebrated nine months later.

In the "Old Country", the nobility of France didn't much care about how the noble "Bastards" were conceived. For many of the upper class, it was considered a rite of passage and concubines were tolerated by wives. If there was a child conceived due to such a liaison, their virile fathers and their noble house found a place in society for them. This attitude did not easily translate itself to Acadie. Some of the noble enterprenneurs, who came to this country, found solace/happiness with indigenous women, of the highest virtue. That ruffled many imperial feathers in France. Although the Crown wanted to Christianize the Mi'kmag/Maliseet peoples, they did not want the "blood royal" to be tainted. Charles St. Étienne de La Tour, a common ancestor to many Acadians, referred to First Nations as "Peuple de ce Pays", according them their due respect while most others referred to them as savages. His first wife was First Nation, as were the wives of many of our ancestors who settled in our historical homelands of La Have, Cape Sable, and the shores of La Baie Francaise (Bay of Fundy) before the English took control with the Treaty of Utrecht, 1713.

After the Proclamation of 1763, we were allowed once again to take up residence in Acadie. Since most of our arable lands had been confiscated, our ancestors the Métis/Acadians, as well as other Acadians and First Nations Peoples tried to locate themselves away from the English conquerors, many in the Tusket River drainage system, from the Pubnico's to the Forks (Quinan) and down into the islands at the mouth of the river, round to the western side just short of Tébok (Chebogue) which had been given to New England Planters, as were the Argyles. The other great influx of our people established the many villages between St. Bernard and Mavilette that became known as "La Ville Francaise", the Clare region of today. Illiteracy combined with having to start again from scratch on less arable lands made our ancestors a cheap workforce for the much more affluent English settlers and businessmen. In order to curry their favor, many Acadians assimilated to the English language and customs, moving into towns like Yarmouth, N. S. It was bad enough being French Frogs/Papists. No one wanted to heap more disdain upon themselves by letting these "*Victors*" know about our Aboriginal roots. In some Acadian families it was never said, in others it was flatly denied that parts of our family trees included Native blood. We wish to address this injustice.

It is not our intention at this time to produce a historical masterpiece that would give all the answers to your questions. Rather, our intention is to bring to light the historical existance of the Métis in Early Acadie, how the Métis/Acadian people learned from one another and put together a society that is still to this day considered unique in Canada. People from this part of the world, the Cajuns from Southeastern United States, the Acadian descendants from Belle Isle en Mer and others who may have journeyed to other parts of the globe after the Expulsion of the Acadians, hopefully, should be able to pick up this document and find out if their family does include Métis/Acadian blood. In this year of the 2004 Congres Mondiale de l'Acadie, many genealogical documents should be available form the various Acadian Family Reunions that should help to complete the puzzle for you.

# Chapter 1.
# The Early Years of "First Contacts"

## A. East meets West or West meets East?

Man by nature is a restless beast. Although you can find many people today who espouse the stay at home attitude that is merely because, especially in the past fifty-sixty years, the world has *shrunk*. All of the amenities of comfort, diet, home, and/or entertainment can be had without having to leave your house. Everything can be ordered electronically, almost from the cradle to the grave. Or you can take the other tact like many of our *Wild Geese* who jet set to the Carribean or other exotic locales to get away from the winter blahs. This was not always the case. Whether coming from East (Asia) or West (Europe), the economics of survival and/or a better life for themselves and their progeny compelled people to move either willingly or forcibly over the past millennia.

It is difficult to state with any accuracy who were the first people to populate Eastern Woodlands and when. This all took place before any written records had been developed. The inescapable truth is that the first settlement of any consequence came from the east. The Mi'kmag, Maliseet, and their relatives have valid claims that place them here at least 5,000 years ago and perhaps as far back as 10,000 years. They have an excellent oral tradition that goes back many generations and this coincides with the receeding of the last Ice Age. The western settlers can't, with any accurate corroboration, go back more than 15-1600 years due to the difficulty of mastering/recording the Atlantic Ocean. They offer the stories of St. Brendan the Navigator and his small group out of Ireland in the Sixth Century. There is no written evidence that actually can substantiate these Irish monks made contact with the indigenous populations of the Americas.. Through the Sagas told by the Scandanavians of Northern Europe, we learn of the famous voyages of Eric the Red who established the early settlement of Greenland. Eric had been banned from Iceland for having murdered another Norse citizen (Circa 980AD).

## B. The Norse Sagas - Stories of Exploration

It is told that his sons, especially, Leif Ericsson, either encouraged by the stories of Bjarny Herjolfson or pushed off course by the winds and currents of the North Atlantic, eventually found them and their company off the Eastern shores of North America. They called the new lands that they "discovered" Vinland, which was probably the Maritimes, south of the Gulf of St. Lawrence. Here there was a abundance of wood, grapes, nuts and self-sown wheat and a much warmer climate than they were used to in Greenland and Iceland. 'The voyages, there were at least three others besides Lief's, were made in late summer which was the only time the ice clogged fjords in Greenland were navigable. This meant that both the out-going and the in-comming voyages had to take place at roughly the same time which tied Lief (and the others) to a voyage of a year's duration."[1]

Attempts at settlement were made at l'Anse aux Meadows in northern Newfoundland.

The Runic Stone in Yarmouth, Nova Scotia, shows that some Norse may have come this far south and perhaps farther. It is the belief of some that there was a Viking village established in Nova Scotia, settled either by Lief Ericson or his brother-in-law, Thorfinn Karlsefne (married to Lief's half-sister Freydis). ".... both, after leaving Newfoundland, made the coast of Nova Scotia. Leif from some part of the coast sailed into the open sea seeking other lands. He may not have gone very far from the low-lying land of Nova Scotia, and being becalmed in foggy weather with the strong currents around the coast, he saw the land of Cape Sable. From that point we easily trace his entrance into Tusket Bay and the river of that same name, where he made his settlement. Thorfinn, on the other hand, gives his route in good form, sailing up a river into a lake, and describes the locality where he spent the winter of 1007-8, at the same place where Lief had made the first settlement, and the old foundations at Vaughne Lake are mute monuments to their settlement there."[2]

However, the Vikings of Scandinavia were not successful in maintaining a permenant settlement on these shores. Why you may ask? The answer lies in a number of circumstances, some of their own making, some not. They did not try to understand the culture and ways of the indigenous peoples who were already populating these "new found lands". They called them Skraeelings, considered them some kind of inferior being, and before long bad blood existed between them. The fierceness of the winters and dwindling of the food supply created sickness and death. 1007, the year that Lief arrived, ultimately ended up being the beginning of the end rather than the beginning of a new homeland for his people. Had these two diverse cultures tried to understand one another as equals, who knows how this "first contact" could have panned out.

I would also like to note that Daniel Paul in his book: "We Were Not the Savages", states that some Mi'kmag were blue eyed and of a fair enough complexion that they were used as "European" spies who could blend in. Perhaps more contact of a social nature was achieved during these early years

*Reg LeBlanc's camp, Meshpok Lake, Quinan. One of several that fill up with Métis/Acadian hunters each fall for the hunt; each spring to fish the lakes and tributaries in our community.*

# Chapter 2.
# The Christopher Columbus Dilemma.
## A. Who Discovered America? Did It Need Discovering?

The next "first contact", the one celebrated in the history books and in many different countries of the world as a religious holiday, resulted when Christopher Columbus sailed the ocean blue from Paulos, Spain, 03 August 1492. New inventions such as the compass and the astrolabe made navigation safer and more practical. Columbus landed on the West Indian island he named San Salvador (Watling's Island) on October 12 thanking God because his crew was ready to mutiny in despair. This year, 2004, Columbus Day in the United States falls on October 11. In Canada we celebrate Turkey Day or Thanksgiving Day on October 11. Which of these two deserves the kudos, the turkey who helps us give thanks to Our Creator for our continued existance on the planet Earth, or the turkey who, in looking for the fabled Northwest Passage to the Orient, claimed for himself, his sovereign Queen Isabella of Castile (Spain), and the Mother Church, dominion over all of these lands and all those who already lived there.

Columbus did not ask the Caribs, the first indigenous people he made contact with, if they wanted a new political system (in which they were to have no say); a new religion that, if not strictly adhered to would condemned them to Hell's fire; or a new culture in which they were to be enslaved and bound like plants to the land.

This Italian navigator who rented himself out to Spanish royalty claimed that he was discoverer of the Americas. I am certain this claim brought chuckles to the Basque

*Taken in Boston Mass., this photo demonstrates just how important the cod fish are, and have been, for the fishers of the Eastern Seaboard.*

fishers and their compatriots from Spain and Portugal who had been fishing the Grand Banks of Newfoundland for many years. Without charts and knowledge of winds, tides, and currents gleaned from some of these fishers, I doubt that the Nina, the Pinta, and the Santa Maria would have left Spain that nice summer day in 1492. These earlier fishers would have weathered out bad storms on the coasts of Nova Scotia and Newfoundland.

They would have landed there for fresh water and resupply if possible. One of these possibilities was to trade with the Mi'kmag who already inhabited these lands and waters. Some old Mi'kmag stories tell of how these Europeans were taught how to dry fish like Cod for transportation back to their homelands rather than their custom of salting the raw fish by layers and hoping that it did not rot before disembarquing in the southwestern ports of Europe. The Catholic Church had about 190 special days that fish was the substitute for meat and even back then, cod was king either as *morue verte* (salted raw) or *morue* sec (sun dried).

# B. A Matter of Religion; The Catholics Get First Crack at "Saving Souls"

God in the form of the Pope in Rome decided to divide the New World between the Spain and Portugal as early as 1494. Once these Catholic countries began the exploitation of Mexico, Central and South America, other European monarchs began to cast an avaricious eye at these lands as well as the unchartered lands and possible oceans to the North. "The conquest of the Aztecs of Mexico by Hernando Cortez and a small force in 1519 brought to light a store of gold and silver such as no European had ever seen before. A few years later, a handful of Spaniards under Francisco Pizarro began the conquest of Peru, where they took from the peaceful Incas quantities of gold and silver that surpassed even the riches of Mexico."[3] The saving of souls in the Americas quickly took a back seat to the mania produced by avaricious people who got mesmerized by these untold riches. The temporal world usurped the spiritual world from the very beginning. This pattern was to continue throughout the early years of contact between the various First Nation peoples and their counterparts from Europe.

Were the Spanish conquistadors solely to blame for their use of the sword to conquer the First Nation peoples who fell under their control? It wasn't until 1537 before the Pope, Paul III, issued his *Sublimus Dei*, which in essence stated that these peoples were human beings and were thus capable of being converted to the Roman Catholic faith.[4] It was a sad day in our history when the man considered God's representative on Earth could rule which humans were worth saving and which weren't. The amazing overriding factor today is that these natives and their conquerors from the more southern climes are the backbone of the Roman Catholic religion today.

The Roman Catholics predominantly captured the souls of the Mi'kmag and Maliseet in Acadia but, once captured, actually did very little for them. This change of religion made it easier for the Europeans to exploit the First Nations who were then engaged in purging their natural surroundings of their former gods: the beaver, the otter, the muskrat, and other *providers* who had served them so well in the past. Beware of he who sells you religion' for the price that you may pay could be too dear!

# C. The Protestants Protest! They Want Colonial Empires Too!

The aspirations to find a passage to the Spice Islands of the Orient remained a priority with the Europeans for centuries to come. Its importance to large populations that were becoming more and more urbanized did not wane. Until refrigeration could preserve foods with very short shelve lives or, at least, spices such as pepper and cinnamon could be used to make unpalatable foods palatable, these needs remained. However, the glitter of gold, silver and other untold riches increased the jealousy of the heads of state in Europe at a time when empire building and the consolidation of power amongst a few royal dynasties was forever changing the map of Europe. The Hapsburgs of Spain and Austria, the Bourbons of France, the Tudors and Stewarts of England,

and the Hohenzollerns of Germany were beginning a winner take all chess game that was to shake Europe to its very foundations over the next three hundred years.

The increased power of some of these monarchies between 1520 and 1660 and the loss of power by petty kings and the nobility of Europe has become known as the Reformation and the Wars of Religion. Having outside powers like the Pope dictate the do's and don'ts of these rising nations, as well as seeing so many properties owned by the Church of Rome being granted as estates by bishops to their "close" relatives,did not sit well with  the ruling class. They felt that the King should appoint the Bishops in his own country. The oppressed lower classes were being left in abject squalor and poverty as the feudal system began collapsing in some countries. A rising middle class, or bourgeoisie, the movers and shakers of capital in these countries, wanted their share of the good life and did not feel that Rome was reflecting neither their morals nor their aspirations. "Practical businessmen had begun to think of poverty as a social evil rather than a saintly virtue"[5]

Martin Luther, an Augustinian Monk, could not shake the fear that had tormented him for years, a fear that there was nothing that he could do in this lifetime to assure him of salvation in the hereafter. As a professor in Wittenberg, Saxony (Germany) around 1515 Luther, reading a verse in St. Paul's Epistle to the Romans to his students, was fascinated by the phrase: *"The just shall live by faith."*[6] His mind translated this small thought that was to help ignite a religious revolution whose repercussions can still be felt today. In a nut shell, he interpreted this part of the Scripture to mean that as long as you kept your faith in God nothing else matters. The directives of the Catholic Church on saving souls, fasting, following the sacraments, buying of dispensations, doing good works or going on pilgrimages, under this form of thought were totally unnecessary. In essence this meant that you take care of number one, both spiritually and in the land of the living.

Certainly, Martin Luther did not preach this earthly part of this dogma, but it had a wide appeal to the followers of other reformers such as John Calvin of Geneva Switzerland. He stated that there should be no church hierarchy. Each congregation should take care of itself by setting up community based churches who picked their own ministers and were not beholding to the government for their existence. Nor were they to be beholden to any greater church authority. All of this was very important to how things were to develop on the Eastern seaboard of North America.

The Colony of New England was developed initially by the Puritans, an offshoot of Calvinism. They considered all the settlers of Acadie and New France to be "Papists". This meant that these French Catholics and any of their converts were heretics whose prolonged presence should be eradicated as soon as possible. The Massachusetts Bay Colony outstripped Acadie in population growth by huge numbers. In 1645, a mere twenty-five years after the first landing of the Pilgrims at Plymouth Rock, there were over 11,000 inhabitants. In major contrast to this, Acadie around 1650 could only muster about 450 permanent settlers from France, a very limited number of them being female.[7]

More would come to Acadie, but never in numbers sufficiant to mount a serious threat to New England. Once this became apparent to our neighbours to the south, a mere two day's sail from the Cape Sable area, encroachment both on land and at sea became inevitable by a people comfortable in their religious beliefs as well as their belief that the Protestant work ethic would make better use of ressources they saw as being underdeveloped by a group who were more often than not political rivals and polluters of the *true* religion. That the Mi'kmaq and Malachite (Maliseet) and their cousins in Maine, the Abanaki were closely allied by faith as well as by religion made the whole matter intolerable. That is why New Englander's were so eager to participate attacking Acadie prior to and very actively during the Deportation of the Acadians.

The French Protestants, known as the *Huguenots*, helped to finance the early settlement of Acadie, hoping to escape religious prosecution in France. The Huguenots followed the doctrines of John Calvin, a fellow Frenchman, who had fled to Geneva, Switzerland where he became a religious and political leader. Calvin believed in simplicity of church service and democratic church organization. His moral code was very strict and he was very intolerant of opposition. Although many of the great Lords had embraced the new faith, France remained a Catholic country and these Lords and their many followers remembered the plots and counterplots that fostered the repeated assassination attempts of Elizabeth I and James I of England.

The unsuccessful Guy Falkes Gunpowder Plot to blow up both protestant King and Parliament is still celebrated in England every November 5. William the Silent of the Netherlands was killed as were Henry III and Henry IV of France. The latter Henry interests us especially because although at one time he was the champion of the *Huguenots* in France, he gave in to the political expediency of giving up religion for a crown. This young Bourbon King of Navarre wed Marguerite of Valois, sister to King Charles IX of France, on 18 August1572. This brought the vast majority of princes and nobles of France together, both Catholic and Huguenot to Paris to witness the wedding and enjoy the following festivities.

These festivities were to serve another purpose. Henry, Duke of Guise and the Queen Mother, Catherine de' Medici, were fanatical followers of the Church of Rome and they saw a golden opportunity to cleanse France of both heretics and political rivals. On August 24, just six days after the royal wedding, a purging of the Huguenot nobility began in Paris that was forever after to be known as the *St. Bartholomew's Day Massacre*. Gaspard de Coligny, Grand Admiral of France, was the prize target. "Coligny's body was thrown from the window (of the Louvre), was dragged through the streets and then cut to pieces; his head was sent as a present to the pope."[8] Other important protestant guests were brought out into the streets and murdered. The Catholic citizens of Paris went on a three day rampage. "The mobs tore women apart and threw babies into the river. Catholic shopkeepers murdered their *Huguenot* competitors, debtors and their creditors - and many men seized the chance to kill their old enemies, *Huguenot* or not."[9]

Of particular interest to us was the killing of Nicolas Mius,

*Plymouth Rock, the immortalized landing point of the Pilgrim Fathers, 1620.*

*The Plymouth Rock Memorial, encasing the original spot.*

Coligny's interpreter and personal assistant. This Swiss emigre had become such a valued member of the Coligny family that Gaspard's widow, his second wife, Jacqueline, adopted Nicolas' son, Claude and raised him as her own, adding one of her territorial titles, d'Entremont, to the Mius name. Claude Antione Mius would go on to marry his benefactor's daughter, Beatrice. They would give life to Sieur Philippe Mius d'Entremont, Baron de Pobumcoup, ancestor to all of the Mius' and d'Entremonts in Acadie. His son, Philippe Mius d'Entremont II, married twice into the Mi'kmag Nation. From his lands in LaHeve his large family spread out to create Métis/Acadian communities, primarily in the Cape Sable region and along the shores of the Bay of Fundy. Not the first Métis/Acadian families to set up in Acadie, they were very prolific and through the years, many would follow in Philippe II's footsteps and marry First Nation women. In so doing they gained a great respect for their Mi'kmag relatives, their way of life, and their concepts of land ownership. The intermarriage and setting up of a new culture by the Mius' and other early families in Acadie will be dealt with in much more depth in the geneological components of this book.

## D. New England, Other English Colonies and the Protestant Work Ethic.

Getting back to the English colonials to the south, throughout the 1600's, they settled colonies from the borders of Maine to the Caribbean. They came to stay and thanks to the financial and military backing of the Crown and other influential entreprenneurs they swept any opposition out of the way. The Dutch lost New Amsterdam, renamed New York in 1664. Plymouth Colony, mentioned earlier, was established in 1620, on some lands that had already been cleared by Pawtucket natives who no longer lived, probably due to smallpox epidemics that spread through the New World by the Spanish. After a few skirmishes with other local Natives, the Pilgrims were fortunate enough to be befriended by two Amerindians. The first native, Samoset, had learned much English by visiting English fishers. After hitting it off well with the Pilgrims, Samoset returned to visit with other tribesmen. One of these men was called Squanto. He chose to remain with his new friends for the rest of his life.

"Squanto showed the Pilgrims where the fish swam, and how to catch them. He showed them where you hunt deer, turkey, and other animals. He showed them where the wild plants and herbs grew - and how to use herbs to make their food taste better. He told them when to plant corn. He showed them how to plant their kernels of corn in little hills, along with three fish in each hill to make the corn grow better."[10] Squanto brokered a peace treaty between Chief Massasoit representing the *Wampanoag Tribe* and Governor John Carver of the Massachussetts Bay Colony.

These two peoples even participated in a yearly Thanksgiving Day feast in the early years, feasting on wild turkey, duck, geese, deer, lobsters, eels, clams, oysters, meat pies, fresh fish, corn, carrots, cucumbers, turnips, onions, cabbage and other plants.[11] This verbal treaty lasted for fifty-four years. By that time, the English had the upper hand in numbers and technology. From then on, the divide, conquer, and confiscate approach to the *Indian Question* was practiced to the extreme. Is it too great a leap to suppose that once they had cleaned out their back yard that the neighbouring papists to the North were to be next?

The British were more advanced in commercial capitalism than the other colonizing nations in the Americas. In order for their mercantilist economic system to work, a balance of trade in which

*Reenactment of British Regulars (Lobster backs) stationed in Boston. It was the cost of billeting these men that began the no taxation without representation attitude, culminating with the Thirteen Colonies going their own way.*

more goods were sold abroad than were brought in was desirable. This appeared to be the case in the Planter/tobacco colonies of Maryland and Virginia where the "*aristocratic*" landowners brought in huge amounts of English manufactured goods, so they could mirror the upper classes of merry old England. These Southern Colonies, having laid all their eggs in one basket (tobacco) ended up with such an imbalance of trade with the Mother Country that by the 1770's *liberty* meant freedom from the English creditors, not the English tyranny of a monarchial system they were trying so much to emulate.

In the New England Colonies, on the other hand, it became apparent at a very early stage of their development that, other than naval stores like spars, pitch, and turpentine, these colonies must survive as "*competitors*" to the Mother Country rather than dumping grounds for British manufactured goods. The New Englanders became fishing magnates, shipbuilders, and maritime shippers and traders, building a strong independent economy that was the envy of many men of great position in England. The Triangle Trade system proved especially lucrative to New England.

In the Triangle Trade system, sugar and molasses were bought in the West Indies, converted into rum in New England. The rum was traded for slaves in Africa and these poor unfortunates were then transported to be sold in the West Indies or the Southern States. Shipping tobacco, as it gained in popularity, to England also was a big money maker for these merchants as was the ongoing coastal carrying trade with other colonies.

Their trading partners included our ancestors in Acadia even though the mother country had imposed laws to the contrary. For them it meant profit, for us, at times, it meant survival. Could this be one of the reasons that *Mother Britannia and the Children* had such a falling-out in 1775???

# Chapter 3.
# The Eastern Woodland People
## A. Where They Came From and Why?

We will take up this story from the French, Acadian and Métis/Acadian prespective a little further along in this book. For now, we are going to focus on the Aboriginal side of the equation and expand on their way of life prior to Columbian *First Contact* and how their story plays out, once the Europeans were here to stay. This we consciously do because they are *our ancestors too* and their story is an integral part of our story.

As has been said before, no one is certain when the First Nations initially crossed over by land from Asia to the Americas on a land bridge which surfaced periodically during the Pleistocene age. People also speculate that there were a number of migrations over a large period of time before this land link, called Beringia, between Siberia and Alaska ceased to exist. What is known is that our other aboriginal brethren, the Innuit, made the perilous crossing by sea in umiacks and kayaks (boats made of waterproofed animal skins) at a later date! Our primary source of aboriginal blood in mainland Acadie or Nova Scotia as it is known today comes from the Mi'kmag People known by the early French as Souriquois, *the salt water men* to differentiate them from the Iroquois, *the fresh water men*. The name Micmac, correctly spelled Mi'kmag is recorded by LaChesnaye in 1676. This proud First Nation says that their name comes from the red earth of their land (take a look in the Annapolis Valley), *Megumawaach*.[12]

Some people in the First Nations would have us believe that their people would have been much better off if they had never seen the first European, let alone at some point or another, have formed alliances with one country or another of these European intruders over the years. The numbers for this argument speak for themselves when one considers that over 85% of the Mi'kmag population died from the diseases that these new contacts brought with them. The big killer diseases included smallpox, measles, influenza, typhus, and tuberculosis. The Mi'kmag and their brethren had no immune system built up to combat these diseases. "The reason for this was that the diseases originated with domesticated animals, which were in abundance in Europe but relatively rare in the New World. Dogs were common among the northern Natives, and llamas used in South America, but neither species was herded in the large groups – such as cattle – necessary for the successful spread of microbes. The conquest of two continents was largely accomplished through inadvertent, but at times deliberate, *germ warfare*."[13]

However, if the clock could successfully be turned back, along similar lines, the Plague would never have come out of Asia to depopulate vast tracts of Europe. The Roman Empire would never have conquered such huge territories in Eurasia by the sword, subjugating yet educating and bringing forth a quest of knowledge and invention that has seen mankind on the verge of outgrowing the parameters of the planet Earth. Without the sharing of knowledge and ideas of both New World and Old, the life of mankind, which is an evolving work of art, may well have stagnated to the point of eventual extinction. Look to the dinosaur, the Neanderthal, Cro-Magnon etc. Intertribal warfare was a fact of life in the America's pre-Columbian where the strong dominated and the weaker etched out an existance or continued to migrate. What is - is! Our ancestors from both sides of the Atlantic have been subjugated at one time or another but we have survived. In achieving survival and renewal, we honour the many that have gone before us.

# B. Culture, Techniques, Religion and Lifestyle.

Trade and commerce have always been a great priority with the pre-Columbian *Natives of the Americas*. "Horticultural Nations traded farm produce for the pelts and meat of hunting countries. Salt and other minerals that were scarce in one territory could be acquired in exchange for products or produce in another..... The infusion of new wares and foodstuffs from Europe soon eroded the century's old, mutually beneficial relationships that the Mi'kmag and other Amerindians had established."[14] The more strain put upon the natural resources the rarer they became. The rarer the pelts became, especially the beaver, the more difficult it became for the Natives to purchase the **essentials** (Guns, alcohol) that the Europeans had brought for trade. I will state at this time that guns do not make murderers but, back then, it sure made murdering easier!!!

"Prior to European settlement the Mi'kmag lived in countries that had developed a culture founded upon three principles: the supremacy of the Great Spirit; respect for Mother Earth; and people power. This instilled in them a deep respect for the laws of the Creator, the powers of Mother Earth and the democratic principles of their society."[15] In the universal view of the Creator, the Mi'kmag were not that dissimilar to the other great monotheistic religions of the world - Christianity, Judaism, Islam, Buddhism etc. This is probably why Chief Membertou and many of his family "converted" to Christianity at Port Royal in the early French period 1613.

The chief of the Mi'kmag was non hereditary. You retained your position as long as the others accepted your judgement and were willing to follow you. A chief was the first amongst equals. With this in mind the "*European*" concepts which separated people into a distinct hierarchy based upon birth, color, race, lineage, religion, profession, wealth, political and other criteria would have seemed to them unbelievable."[16] It made no more sense than Chief Membertou walking through the gates of London, England, claiming the city for himself.

# C. Food Gathering and Farming.

The pre Columbian Mi'kmag lived in a remarkably structured early Stone Age civilization. Their villages were, for the most part, small. They cultivated gardens using implements of wood and/or bone. The main crops were corn, squash, beans, sunflowers, pumpkins, and tobacco. The forests increased their bounty with wild fruits, berries, greens, seeds, and nuts. The Mi'kmag people were also very adept at tapping the sap from the maple trees. This sap was then converted into syrup and sugar. "Menus included a wide variety of foods, of which many, such as maple sugar, popcorn, hominy, succotash, wild rice, and persimmon bread, were *adopted* by the early white settlers."[17]

Although the abovementioned sounds like a great variety of foods, these were not the main diet of the Mi'kmag and other tribes of the Eastern Woodlands. Following the wild game, combined with the possible encroachment of other tribes on their homelands, were the main motivators for the Mi'kmag settling in the Northeastern extremities of North America. The animals of this area and the fish from both the fresh and salt water sources provided the staples of their diet. This is why they developed such mobile communities that could easily be dismantled to follow the game or fish during the appropriate seasons. Large and small game such as bear, deer, moose, rabbit, beaver, wild pigeon, turkey, partridge, quail and a large variety of water fowl were hunted with bow and arrow and wooden and stone headed clubs. Their ingenious method of felling trees was a combination of covering a small section with clay/wet earth and burning around the exposed areas until the tree could be toppled with a stone axe.[18] It became very important that the keepers of the fire in each community be diligent at their job. Fire provided them with heat for cooking, for warmth, for light, for protection against outside interference, two-legged or four –legged. Fires were also instrumental on ceremonial occasions, from the torture of the enemy to the purification of tribal members.

# D. Modes of Travel, Inventions, and Medicines.

Mother Nature supplied them with cooking utensils made of wood or folded birch bark. Black pottery was used for cooking and storing food. Baskets were made from the splints and fibers of black ash, linwood or basswood. Rolling the basswood fibers in the palm of your hand, twisting them together, against the naked thigh or calf produced a thread that could be used for weaving belts, tump lines (slings), and fastening weaponry. Bows were fashioned of hickory, orangewood, oak and ash. The arrows were pointed with heads of chipped flint, sharpened bone or claws. Birch bark had many uses besides cooking. The birch bark canoe became the workhorse of the Northeast, just as the water systems, the rivers, lakes and oceans became their highways. These canoes made of strips of birch bark stitched together around a light wooden frame and waterproofed with pitch were very light, easily repaired and could be made of various sizes.

The small one/two man canoe could move over land (portages) and sea quite easily but the larger 14/20 man canoe is the beast of labour that could carry over 3000 pounds of supplies, housing, or furs vast distances very economically. They served the Mi'kmag and their other aboriginal neighbors well in the beginning but these vessels were also quickly adopted by the European newcomers to exploit the fur trade and open up the country for the waves and waves of other newcomers looking to settle on "free" land.

The Mi'kmag, like other First Nations, had a vastly different notion of the land than did the newcomers. Just as hoarding and greed had little use in the Amerindian way of life, individual land ownership was unconscionable. "The People lived wherever they found what they liked to eat. Their villages might be pitched where the fishing was good, or near hunting grounds they and their ancestors had always known. The land they used was not owned by men and women but was held in a communal relationship with the spirits of the forests."[19] During the summer months, they pursued the salmon, cod, alewives, clams, lobster and other seafoods to the shores where they ate their fill and cured the rest for the upcoming winter months. In the fall, they mostly removed themselves inland where they could hunt the moose (often using dogs when snow permitted), caribou, black bear, and other denizens of the forest. Setting up camp in the shelter of the forest rather than on the windswept coasts also made good sense - and common sense is what these people were all about. The coming of spring also saw these people drawing the *waters* of the maple, which they used as both a sweetener and a medicine.

Nicolas Denys had this to say about the dietary habits of the Mi'kmag and their longevity prior to the introduction of European diseases: "There were formerly a much larger number of Indians than at present. They lived without care, and never ate salt or spice. They drank only good soup, very fat. It was this that made them live long and multiply much. They often ate fish, especially seals to obtain the oil, as much for greasing themselves as for drinking; and they ate the Whale which frequently came ashore on the coast, especially the blubber, on which they made good cheer. Their greatest liking is for grease; they ate as one does bread, and drink it liquid...Cacamo was their greatest delicacy. In order to make it , the women: made the rocks red hot... collected all the bones of the Moose, pounded them with rocks upon another larger, reducing them to powder; then they placed them in their kettle and made them boil well. This brought out a grease that rose to the top of the water, and they collected it with a wooden spoon. They kept the bones boiling until they yielded nothing more, and with such success that from the bones of one Moose, without counting the marrow, they obtained five to six pounds of grease as white as snow, and as firm as wax. It was this which they used as their entire provision for living when they went hunting."[20]

Modern science has proven that their'low stress, high fat (the right kind) diet, and seasonally nomadic lifestyle'were ideally suited to the Mi'kmag and their brethren for many, many generations. That their famous chief, Membertou, lived to be over one hundred years old does not in any way appear to be an exaggeration. The fact that he was taller than average and sported a beard makes one wonder about the components of Membertou's family tree. Examples of a disease like measles decimating Aboriginal people can still be found in the 20th Century when the Americans built the Alaska Highway to defend Alaska in 1942. The ensuing measles epidemic killed many Tllngit who had not yet experience such diseases until thousands of American soldiers, including black regiments of construction engineers from the South showed up for the next two winters, unwittingly spreading measles and other diseases the Tllngit had not yet acquired immunity too.

Had it not been for the French *newcomers* the story of our Métis/Acadian forbearers would never have had a beginning - hence no existence. The Mi'kmag considered their country to include the Maritime Provinces plus a substantial portion of Eastern Quebec. Fate saw to it that this is where some of the first French colonists set sail for on *Le Don de Dieu* out of LeHavre, France on 7 April1604. This group was headed by Pierre de Gua, Sieur de Monts, who brought with him both Catholics and Huguenots as participants. The geographer, explorer, who accompanied him, was Samuel de Champlain, a man with prior experience in the New World and whose humongous efforts left him known throughout history as the Father of New France. But that is another story.

On May 8, they arrived in Green Bay, Lunenbourg County, Nova Scotia. "Champlain drew a detailed map of the area where they landed, naming it Port de La Hêve. He named the cliff Cap de La Hêve after the last cape they saw as they headed out onto the Atlantic Ocean from France...The first Catholic and Protestant services in Canada were held on board the vessel the second day it was anchored in the bay."[21] (Sieur de Monts, himself a nobleman of the reformed faith, read the service for the Huguenot members under his care). La Have, as it is now known, is a primary historical site for the Eastern Woodland Métis Nation. A Mi'kmag community existed there when these first French landed there and a *Métissage* or mixing of Aboriginal and French blood was to happen on many occasions there up till the beginning of **Le Grand Dérangement of 1755.**

The Land of the Mi'kamg was divided into seven distinct districts (see accompanying map). They controlled the activities of the small villages (50-500) in their area. Each district had a Chief and Council, comprising village Chiefs and Elders (of both sexes). They decided on peace or war, hunting areas, fishing areas and any local disputes. All members of the Council had the right to be heard, whether in District Council or Grand Council, officiated by a Grand Chief selected from amongst the District Chief, retaining this position for as long as he maintained the respect of the others. "Mi'kmag Districts also belonged to a larger association known as the Wabanaki Confederacy, which had been formed by the northeastern First Nations for the purpose of providing mutual protection from aggression by Iroquoian and other hostile Nations. The Confederacy continued to function until the early 1700's, at which time the decimation of its member Nations by disease and wars with the English caused its demise."[22]

Religion had great importance to the Mi'kmag People. They saw the **Great Spirit** as the initiator of all things animate and inanimate. "He encompassed all positive attributes - love, kindness, compassion, knowledge, wisdom etc., and that He was responsible for all existence and was personified in all things – rivers, trees, spouses, children, friends etc. No initiatives were undertaken without first requesting His guidance. His creations, Mother Earth and the Universe, were accorded the highest respect. Religion was blended into daily life - it lived."[23]

With regard to marriages, persons could not marry closer then second cousins in order to

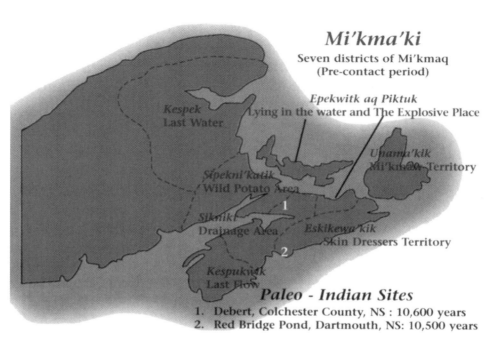

**Mi'kma'ki**
Seven districts of Mi'kmaq
(Pre-contact period)

*Epekwitk aq Piktuk*
Lying in the water and The Explosive Place

Kespek
Last Water

Unama'kik
Mi'kmaw Territory

Sipekni'katik
Wild Potato Area

Siknikt
Drainage Area

Eskikewa'kik
Skin Dressers Territory

Kespukwik
Last Flow

**Paleo - Indian Sites**
1. Debert, Colchester County, NS : 10,600 years
2. Red Bridge Pond, Dartmouth, NS: 10,500 years

preserve strong blood lines. Plural marriages were accepted but not the rule. If two married people could not get along, *divorce* was expected rather than frowned upon because their misery was contagious and the severing of ties would free both parties to select another mate. The children of the first marriage would be adopted by the new husband.Children with no parents were taken care of by the village. "The relationship (between man and woman) had to be carried on according to civilized customs. The Mi'kmag and the Acadians came to an understanding in this regard and, later on, as social exchanges developed, a great number of intermarriages took place."[24] These strong bonds between the early French adventurers, courreurs de bois, and the Mi'kmag were to create the early Métis / Acadian families who were instrumental in the creation/maintenance of the settlements in the Baie Francaise region, spreading out primarily north from Port Royal initially and going cross land to the LaHeve and the Cape Sable areas.

Although not all French settlers married Native women, even those who didn't get along well with their new neighbours. The Mi'kmag people didn't fear these newcomers because they, the Natives, had vastly superior numbers and could have terminated this relationship at the very beginning if they had wanted to. These newcomers did not want to set up hurdles of superiority, dominance or demands of land that would threaten the age accepted ways of the Native People. Many of them were young, in their early or mid teens. During this age when the average life expectancy in Europe was thirty, one third or more of a ship's company were rookies who may have hired themselves out as indentured servants. Once their three year term had expired they were given the option of remaining or going back home. Some went back, but many stayed.

The democratic ways of the Mi'kmag with their overtures of friendship saw many a young man get involved with the fur trade and the life of adventure that it conjured up. If you were a young man living in France in the seventeenth century your choices were limited. You could become a tenant farmer and spend your entire life working on someone else's land for a fraction of what your labor has brought forth. The almost constant wars that were being waged to sooth the pride of an absolute monarch could demand that you become cannon fodder for their opponent's army or navy. The Plague and other diseases that swept through Europe might seal your fate and those of your family, if you could scrape up the wherewithal to start a family.

Scurvy eroded the numbers of the early settlers and terrified those who remained until for the second time (Jacques Cartier and his crew were shown how to cure this disease by the Natives back in the 1530's), the Mi'kmag People demonstrated how boiling the bark of the white cedar and drinking this substance would revitalize your body and purge the scurvy. With sickness in abeyance, chances of owning your own land, riches to be made on the fur trade and available young women who were capable of taking care of you better than you could take care of yourself, it is not surprising that so many brave hearts chose a life away from the religious wars that were tearing their homelands apart. "It must be remembered that the letters patent (Royal authorization to get involved in the New World to De Monts, as well as to Poutrincourt and Razilly, involved Christianizing the Indians. Consequently religion was one of the Raison D'être of Acadia, and so it is not surprising that the religious aspect was always important to the Acadians."[25]

## E. Attitudes Towards French, English Before Governance.

The few non-Catholics who wished to settle and marry in Acadie would convert to Catholicism at the time of the wedding. This included some Dutch and Basque men.

Mi'kmag maids who married an Acadian would accept her husband's religion if that were his wish and would faithfully raise their children as Catholics with a little help and explanation that would come from the village Elders and the itinerant Priest. One bone of contention that genealogists have with the recording (if recorded) of these marriages was that the presiding Priest would list the bride as *Inconnu* or give them a name like *Marie Amerindienne*. It becomes very difficult to determine ancestry with these diminutive pronunciations, a cultural bias of the times. Sometimes these priests forgot that they were the servants of God and not the Master himself.

Remember, the Mi'kmag had their own well developed monotheistic religion. In many ways it paralleled Christian beliefs. The **GREAT SPIRIT** overlooked all other things happening in the Universe and He too was a God of peace. This was one of the main reasons that the Mi'kmag converted so easily to Christianity. They were not interested in following the Roman Catholic Church teachings, Bible and Script. They did understand that the *Big Picture* was the same for both peoples and a lot of them did convert before practice of only selling firearms to Catholic Indians was instituted.

Mainland Acadie or Nova Scotia was nominally under British control after 1713 but to the Mi'kmag, the Métis/Acadians and the Acadians that did not mean much. Port Royal had been renamed Annapolis Royal but it only had a small military detachment as did Canso. These troops were here merely to demonstrate British dominion not to enforce British dominance. At times they had to rely on the local inhabitants for the basic needs of survival and woe to him who dared travel far from the Fort without an escort. The wars of Europe kept looking like they were going to spill over into Acadie and the Acadians, especially the native born sons, whether of mixed blood or not, did not want to become embroiled in a fight that might see them killing their former countrymen. The Mi'kmag had a perhaps clearer perception of what was to come if the British floodgates were to open up and sweep all before their path. These People of the Red Earth kept up a constant harassment of the British outposts. They also warned their Acadian brethren neither to submit to British domination nor to supply them with men and arms at their own parrel.

The British tried to buy the Mi'kmag off with a Treaty in 1752. "It is agreed that the said Tribe of Indians shall not be hindered from, but have free liberty of hunting and fishing as usual and that if they shall think a Truckhouse needful at the River Chibenaccadie, or any other place of their resort they shall have the same built and proper Merchandize, lodged therein to be exchanged for what the Indians have to dispose of and that in the mean time the Indians shall have free liberty to bring to Sale to Halifax or any other settlement within this Province. Skins, feathers, fowl, fish, or any other thing they shall have to sell, where they shall have the liberty to dispose thereof to the best advantage."[26] This type of treaty was set up to lull the Mi'kmag and their allies into a false sense of security by guaranteeing their hunting and fishing lands until British feats of arms could settle this issue for once and for all.

# F. Life Under The British Empire, Post 1763.

The die was cast for the Mi'kmag. What they perceived to be a war of attrition, a war of survival and way of life was swept out the door by the conclusion of the Seven Year's War. The Proclamation of 1763 spoke of setting up a Native Nation west of the Allegheny Mountains to sooth the Tribes of the Ohio and Mississippi River drainage systems. Nothing was said about the Mi'kmag, who had never surrendered their lands to anybody but now saw it being usurped by the victorious British. Some of them had been deported with the Acadians, some had drowned on route. Those who remained were forced to sign submissive treaties that would see the erosion of not only their lands but also their ways of life - the freedom to roam the woods and waters of now and forevermore...

Many of the Métis/Acadians felt the same way and, as we shall see, they would have to go to Halifax, hat in hand, depending on the leniency or benevolence of British aristocrats and/or soldiers. The lands that they had cultured in this province were bargaining chips to bring in primarily New England settlement. To the Mi'kmag and the Acadians the fox had been put into the chicken house and their best bet would be to settle as far away from the chicken house as would be economically feasible. In the long run, the Acadians would have some choice. For our brothers the Mi'kmag, the choices were to be mostly made for them. Isn't civilization a great thing!

Acadia had been handed back and forth between France and England at least six times in less than one hundred years before being finally ceded to England for good in 1713. "In 1650 the whole population of Acadie was about four hundred people and made up 45 to 50 families of French origin living around Port Royal and La Have, plus a nomadic group of about 60 men, soldiers, hired hands, and coureurs de bois working in the fur trade for LaTour and Nicolas Denys. Most Acadians can trace their origins from one of those fifty families."[27] The restrictions of self-development and trade by the *Absolute Monarchy* of France prevented Acadia, New France and the vast territorial Mississippi/Ohio River tracts from ever achieving a population density that would enable them to forever be viable bulwarks to the imperial expansion of the British.

"New France developed slowly, as merchants and fur-traders penetrated to the Great Lakes and Samuel de Champlain explored Hudson Bay and tried to build a settlement at the inhospitable Bay of Fundy. In 1608, Quebec was founded and Frenchmen, accompanied by Jesuit missionaries, and in alliance with Indian tribes, pushed inland and southwards. Inevitably, they were to clash with the English, both in the south and the north, where Charles II encouraged the Hudson's Bay Company to take a share of the lucrative fur trade. Although the area settled by the French was vast, it was sparsely inhabited, for the French showed less enthusiasm for colonization than the English and support from their home was often half-hearted and sporadic."[28] This quote comes from an educational encyclopedia published in London, England, in the 1970's. The nearest it comes to mentioning Acadia is Champlain's attempt to build a settlement at the inhospitable Bay of Fundy. In an encyclopedia meant to educate young Englanders, this is an apt description of the importance given now as much as "back then" to the role Acadia played in the game of empire from the English point of view. We were mere pawns, to be given up, to be traded, and in the end to be mostly forgotten.

It must be said in Charles II's defense, that he was in favour of religious tolerance in his domains. Parliament under Oliver Cromwell had lopped off his father's head and he had to play according to their game plan to keep his own throne. To limit Parliament's influence over him, Charles II accepted a large sum of money from Louis XIII, the remainder of his dowry promised in 1625 when he had wed Louis' sister, Henriette-Marie. More attention will be given to this detail later in our story. This allowed him some leeway to live life as he saw fit in an era of Bubonic Plague, Small Pox (this disease killed his brother, Henry), and the Great London Fire that was blamed on the Catholics the following year. Although he was the titular head of the Church of England, Charles died a Catholic. His brother and successor, James II who also reconverted to Catholicism, creating another royal crisis in England that saw William of Orange and his wife Mary, James' Protestant daughter, invited from Holland to take over the crown.

The War of the Spanish Succession (1702-1713), known in North America as Queen Anne's War, was instigated by the Sun King Louis X1V, a clash between the Bourbons and the Hapsburgs for the throne of Spain. The Protestant monarchs, especially England did not want to see these two Catholic countrys under the same king. The French were defeated by Marlborough's combined forces at Blenheim. The Treaty of Utrecht, 1713, saw the Spanish throne go to Louis' grandson, Philippe, with the understanding that he could never become king of France. One of France's pawns, lost for the last time, was mainland Acadie. It is amusing to see how the *royal mind* worked. Louis XIV epitomizes the belief that the king derives his *Absolute Power from God and God alone*. This belief was purely predestination on behalf of a Catholic monarch who fought so many battles against Protestant countries that espoused predestination for everyone. He and his country paid dearly for his follies.

France retained Cape Breton Island (Isle Royale), Prince Edward Island (Isle St.Jean), New France (Quebec), the Ohio River trading system and Louisiana. Our ancestors were given the right to leave their homes and move over to lands still under the French flag. Put yourself in their position. Given a chance to remain in the land where you were born, where you had buried your loved ones, where you were living in harmony with both the Mi'kmaq and nature. Would you have willingly uprooted the young, the old, the infirm along with whatever you could carry to start again especially on Isle Royale where the Fortress Louisbourg showed just like a matador waving a red flag at the British. As long as our people were not forced to bare arms against the French and could maintain their religion they were mostly content to live under the Union Jack of Britain.

As mentioned earlier, during this period leading up to the Deportation and the French Indian War (1756-1763), until the establishment of Halifax in 1749, the British had only two outposts of any consequence in Acadia - Annapolis Royal and Canso. Left in a Catch 22 situation, the troops needed the Acadians as a source of supply and a buffer against the Mi'kmaq, who saw the writing on the wall if England was to persevere. On the other hand, the Acadians vastly outnumbered the British garrisons and the possibility always existed (in their minds) that if the Acadians rose in rebellion with the Mi'kmag, chances were that the troops would be wiped out. Lieutenant-Governor Thomas Caulfield put these fears to words: "If the French leave, we will never be able to support English families here, and protect them from the harassment by the Indians, who are the worst enemies imaginable."[29] The Acadians, by and large, became known as the Neutral French and they were happy to keep things that way.

"Acadians had begun to identify themselves as a separate people. Along with their Indian friends, they were the only permanent settlers of the huge territory now known as the Maritimes. They were no longer French from France. They had their own political and social organization, their own imaginative ways of cultivating land along the Bay of Fundy and they had become a fairly affluent group compared to the average French peasants. They had grown used to freedom and space. They had learned to trade with New England without bothering too much about who might officially be in control of Acadie. Some of them had become very powerful business people."[30] All of this was to change when Governor Charles Lawrence arbitrarily set into motion the Expulsion of the Acadians -Métis/Acadians, non-Métis/Acadians, and the Mi'kmag of Acadie.

*George's Island in Halifax Harbor today.*
*It was a living hell for our people incarcerated there during the Expulsion years.*

# Chapter 4.
# The Early Years of Métis/Acadian Settlement.

## A. Getting a Grip on Acadian Soil

Although the beaver was considered "king" of the fur trade industry that developed with the founding of settlements in Acadie in 1604, the cod had been "*king*" for over one hundred years prior to these early attempts at colonization. After the rape of Acadie's natural ressources and once the conflicts of empire had been resolved once and for all in Great Britain's favor, cod was once more to superimpose itself over the beaver and for the next three hundred years, it had much to say how our ancestors were to survive in this New World. The fishers of Normandy, Breton, and the Basques had been preoccupied with the fish of the Grand Banks, making two trips each year. From late January to April /May they would brave the North Atlantic to bring in the early catch which would bring in the best prices. They would about-turn and return to the Banks as quickly as the seas would allow them and return for their second trip.

As was mentioned earlier, *morue verte* and *morue sec* (salt or dried cod) were in huge demand and hundreds of boats made these trips on an annual basis. Contraband cargo in the form of seven savages made their way to Rouen as early as 1507. "By 1519 the French, the Portuguese, and the English had set up depots on Newfoundland, on the Acadian peninsula, on Cape Breton Island, and on the St.Lawrence River."[31] No permanent settlements, but you can bet your boots that there was a fair amount of trading going on between these Europeans and the indigenous population. No doubt, from time to time, intercourse of a sexual nature also entered the picture.

In this era of vast *Colonization* of the civilizations of New World and the hither-to-known ancient empires of the East (India, China etc.), King Henri IV, a man of tolerant views for his time, granted to Sieur De Monts, as mentioned before, what has come to be known as Acadie plus all the lands situated between the 40-46th lines of latitude. "De Monts was granted fishing and fur trading rights on the condition that he settle and cultivate the land, prospect for mines, and bring about the conversion of the native peoples...It excluded the St.Lawrence River but it included the entire eastern seaboard from present day New Jersey to Cape Breton."[32]

After making La Have, this being the beginning of summer, De Monts, Champlain, Jean De Biencourt (Sieur De Poutrincourt and De Saint-Just, a Catholic favorite of King Henry IV), and their other companions skirted southern Nova Scotia. After a short stop at Port Rossignol (Liverpool), they made camp for a number of weeks at Port Mouton (so named for the accidental drowning of a sheep in this harbor), to revitalize and to refurbish their water and supplies. They rounded Cape Sable Island, eventually passing the many islands at the mouth of the Tusket River.

To the largest island, Champlain gave the name Saint Martin. On today's maps, you may read Big Tusket, but to this author who maintains a summer camp there as well as all other true Acadians, the name remains St. Martin. Many of these locales, new to these Europeans, were given names of saints, other religious names, or the names of *important* people. Giving a place a saint's name on his birthday helped to keep the records straight on any given year. It should be noted that the English only adopted the Gregorian calendar in

1752. This caused a few days' discrepancy between the records kept by England or other Europeans before this date (Leap Year numbers were the culprits).

These men then entered the Bay of Fundy (La Baie Francaise), took a look at St.Mary's Bay, and eventually decided to cross over to the western shores of Fundy to settle in for the winter at what is today known as Dorchet's Island at the mouth of the Saint Croix River. This choice was not to prove a wise one. Picked for military reasons; easily defendable by cannon, the harshness of the North American winter was almost to prove their undoing.

What the freezing northeasterlies did not do, scurvy and starvation did. By the spring, those forty-four, who had been fortunate enough to survive (out of 79), looked to find a more hospitable location. They found it by sailing east across the Bay to Port Royal. St. Croix was dismantled and brought to the Annapolis Basin and placed in a wind protected location with plenty of access to food and water. "The Habitation constructed in Port Royal in 1605 under the supervision of Champlain served as a comfortable shelter for a small group of men for two years.....de Mons and Champlain learned a great deal from the native people that helped them to survive in the New World."[33] Champlain spent the winters of 1605-6 in Port Royal while Poutrincourt spent the winter of 1605 home in France looking for new men and supplies to help bolster the new fort. 1606 saw him return to Acadie with a goodly number of aristocrats and artisans ready for adventure. Poutrincourt's son, Charles, accompanied him as did his cousin from Champagne, Claude Ste Étienne de La Tour (Governor of Dieppe), and his fourteen year old son, Charles. Louis Hébert, apothecary and horticulturalist came as did Marc Lescarbot, a lawyer with many accomplishments, not the least, his "Histoire de la Nouvelle France".

Lescarbot first cast eyes on our Mi'kmag brethren at Campseau where Poutrincourt laid anchor. He writes: "Meanwhile the two longboats came up, one manned with savages, the other by Frenchmen from St.Malo who were fishing off Canso. The savages showed the greater diligence, for they arrived first...and I admired their fine shape and well formed faces. One of them made his excuses that on account of the inclemency of the weather he had not brought his beautiful beaver robe. He wore only a piece of coarse red frieze, with Matachiaz (Decorations) around his neck and wrists, above his elbows, and at his waist."[34] The year 1607 saw De Monts monopoly was revoked in 1607. Poutrincourt managed to take over where DeMonts left off but the climate in France was rapidly changing. Religious tolerance was being squeezed out of the mother country and both New France and Acadie would feel this pressure. The Catholics were winning the war of religion in the home country, especially when the Jesuits, a fanatical militant order of Spanish origins, dealt themselves into the game.

Saving the souls of those heretics who had *strayed from the true Faith* was supposed to be their chief occupation but this order *allowed* itself to be played from a political point of view as well. Having them in the new colony that proclaimed tolerance was more than Pourtrincourt could handle, especially after the assassination of Henry IV by a fanatic Catholic named Francois Ravaillac, on 14 May1610. Had all the Bourbon's who followed Henry been more open minded with regards to religion, their dynasty might have survived without the many intrigues plied against them throughout their reigns.

Henry's premature death was to give the Jesuits Ennemond Masse and Pierre Briard almost carte blanche to aggressively pursue their agenda of temporal interference in Acadie, their sponsor being the widowed Queen, Marie de Medici. Never again would the Huguenots have a chance to evolve peacefully under the *Fleur-de-Lis* of France. The independently rich financial backer young Charles de Biencourt had to deal with on behalf of his father was Antionette de Pons, Marquess of Guercheville. When her Jesuits complained of non-compliance with the Poutrincourt family, she withdrew her support entirely and decided to set up a new colony.

Unwittingly or not, Guercheville's meddling began the process of wars on the Eastern Seaboard that would eventually self destruct her aspirations all-together. Her Jesuits set sail on *Le Fleur de Mai* in early 1613, went to Port Royal to strip that colony of anything that was not tied down (great stuff for men of God), and then proceeded to Mont-Deserts de Pentagoet - today's Penobscot, Maine. They gave this new mission the name Saint Sauveur (Holy Savior). This shows you how much a name means. Little more than a month had passed when Samuel Argall, the Virginia Company's enforcer, came up from Jamestown to prevent encroachment on Virginia's boundaries. Saint Sauveur was within the territories claimed by the English and it had to go. "He put the torch to the colony, killed anyone who resisted, and took a handful of prisoners back to Virginia on a captured French ship, and set Father Masse and fifteen others adrift in an open boat (from which they would be rescued by fishermen)."[35]

## B. Charles de Biencourt and Charles de La Tour: Survival Amongst the Mi'kmag – The Mixing Begins.

Knowing the whereabouts of Port Royal, Argall decided to make a clean sweep of things. Arriving in Port Royal early October, Argall razed the settlement while most of its occupants were either out in the fields or in the interior with the two Charles (de Biencourt and de La Tour) trading with the Mi'kmag. "Biencourt and his colonists immediately began building temporary shelters, working against time as winter drew near, storing artichokes and other native roots and vegetables. Hunting, never a sport, became a battle of survival as quarters and sides of moose were put aside. Luckily for the settlers, Argall had not found a flour mill farther up the Annapolis. Fortunately too the Micmacs shared what they could."[36] The Mi'kmag are a very stoic people who, in order to survive with dignity, had early learned to accept the inevitable and carry on. This seemed to rub off on the young Frenchmen in their midst. Charles de Biencourt, his cousin and several of their associates remained in Port Royal with their allies to continue with their plans while his father returned to France seeking to re-supply and rebuild.

The Poutrincourts, father and son, were never to see each other again. Jean de Poutrincourt perished fighting in the religious wars of the Old Country and his son kept his group of about twenty busy in the fur trade with the aboriginals. "Biencourt set up a series of observation posts along the coast and used them to signal ships when he had furs to exchange for ammunition and other provisions (Norman, Breton and Basque fishermen). In 1616 he was able to ship some 25,000 pelts back from trading posts at Port Royal, Cape Sable, Penobscot and the St. John River."[37] Sieur Claude St. Étienne de La Tour must have hopped into one of these fishing vessels, for he also sailed back to France looking for new blood, new capital and support of a more positive nature by the French Crown.

The Virginians, wanting to get rid of Acadie in its weakened state, sent Samuel Argall on another *tour of duty* in 1619. Argall laid waste to Saint-Sauveur, Saint Croix, and Port Royal. Homes and supplies up in smoke, Charles de Biencourt and his friends once again looked upon their Mi'kmag relatives for support. Many of the young Frenchmen, including both Charles', had married into the Maliseet or Mi'kmag Nations by this time. As Noel Knockwood, B.A., Elder, stated in his December, 1995, presentation, THE MÉTIS NATION – *A Free and Independent People to 1885*: Native peoples who trapped the coveted furs were not always friendly, and the wilderness environment was often hostile. These women ensured the survival of the European men by supplying them with appropriate clothing such as moccasins, snowshoes, and buckskin jackets, food from the wild and family ties to Native groups and trading partners.

This band of *courreurs de bois*, in essence, was the progenitor of the first Métis in Acadia. Charles de Biencourt joined his ancestors at the age of 31 in 1624. To the best of my knowledge, he bequeathed the Seigneury given to his father by De Monts to his cousin and closest associate, Charles de La Tour, then 27. Young de La Tour moved their headquarters to Cape Sable in order to be in closer proximity to his European lifeline, the fishermen. David Lomeron, backed by La Rochelle's Huguenots, was the merchant they depended upon. The trading post in Cape Sable, on Chebogue Point, was named after this enterprising middleman who provided an essential service during unstable times.

Charles posted two letters to France in 1627, one to King Louis XIII, the other to Cardinal Richelieu, requesting from both of these mighty men, an official commission and supplies that would allow him to defend Acadie. "He explains that because of the destruction of Port Royal by the English, he and the other Frenchmen have been living and dressing like (les peuples du pays) the people of this land."[38] This is as close as he gets to talking about the Métis/Acadian families that are beginning to form. Someone reading between the lines could understand that de La Tour purposefully did not use the term savages, generally used by Europeans, when referring to First Nation Peoples. The outbreak of another French-English war in the same year prevented, let us say for discussion's purposes, Richelieu from immediately granting this request. The Cardinal did, however, found the Company of One Hundred Associates whose mandate was to populate the colonies with French settlers. He was taking a page from the Great Britain's game book. Almost all of the English colonies had been established by private enterprise. We still maintain today that if you want a business to fail, let the government take it over. This new French company had many powerful backers, including one of the Cardinal's cousins, Isaac de Razilly, whom we shall get to in a little while.

## C.    Nicolas (Claude) Turgis de Saint Étienne de La Tour – a Man for All Ages

First we are going to look into the wheelings and dealings of a master survivor in the aristocratic world of seventeenth century Europe –Nicolas (Claude) Turgis de Saint Étienne de La Tour, Charles' father. If this father had been less of an able diplomat (some people use other words), the de La Tour aspirations in Acadie would have been short lived. Claude was an adventurer and a charmer who remained on top of his game till the later stages of his life. On his way back to his son after protecting de La Tour interests at the Court of King Louis, being assured assistance from the One Hundred Associates, Claude became part of the booty from the privateering escapades of the Kirke brothers.

Sieur de La Tour, once again taking a fall and landing on his feet, befriended David Kirke to such an extent that he was introduced to the Court of King Charles when they arrived in London. There he won the favors of one of the Queen's attendants, Marie, widow of Francois Gaudart, attorney of Chatelet, France. The Lady became so infatuated with this ageing courtier that she agreed to not only become his wife but also to follow him to Acadie. She thought that she was getting better than what she got, probably because her new husband had made a deal with Sir William Alexander, a Scottish nobleman who had been granted Acadie (he was to name Nova Scotia) by the King's dead father, King James VI of Scotland and King James I of England . The deal was to be de La Tour's knowledge of the aforementioned Acadie combined with talking his son, Charles, into giving up Fort Saint Louis (Villagedale/White Sand Beach, Shelburne Co.) The de La Tours would each receive a piece of New Scotland and a Knight's Baronet Title from King Charles.   Sieur Claude got the best of that deal. The Baronet titles were granted to both father and son but Charles de La Tour, for good or for bad, had thrown in his lot with France and he wished to remain loyal to the Bourbons.

Madame Claude de La Tour accepted her fate graciously and, like one of the American president's wives in the 1990's, stood by her man. The La Tours did not remain estranged for long. A nice home was built for Sieur Claude and his wife just outside the walls of the fort at Cape Sable and they were amply provided for by the son. So says Nicolas Denys who visited them in 1635. The house was outside the palisades, so that Charles could not be accused of harboring an enemy of the State. Eventually, Claude would renew his allegiance to the French Crown. Taken out of the political game, Sieur/Baronet Claude had secured some wiggling room for his son that would be invaluable to him in the not to distant future.

It is well worth mentioning that Claude de La Tour has been viewed by many as having been a practicing Huguenot when he first left France for the New World. Born circa 1560, Sieur de La Tour had contracted his first marriage in the early 1590's with Marie de Salazar, daughter of Hector (2) de Salazar and Antoinette de Courcelles. The Salazar family was very prominent in France. Its roots go back to include King Louis IX, and includes other close familial ties to the Saint-Étienne, the Bourbon-Montpensiers, the Montmorency-Lavals and the de Lespinasse. This marriage gave Claude a son, obviously, Charles, who was born in 1593 in Champagne, France. Marie was not destined to remain with them for long. She passed away sometime in 1602. Probably in 1608/09 there was nothing keeping him in France now that his son was seventeen, old enough to be considered a man in that epoch. That Charles was raised a Catholic in his adolescent years we know. Just how much religion affected him is difficult to say. As situations in his life evolved, I believe that he went with the flow, reminding the English that his father was a Protestant if that was in his best interest or reminding the French that he was a baptized son of Rome if that could carry the day.

One more aspect of Claude de La Tour should be mentioned. He had married a second wife, Marie Guesdon, daughter of Claude Guesdon and Madeleine Ogeron, in 1615 while he was back in Paris. Not much more is known to this author about this union. One must assume that Mme. Guesdon de La Tour died prematurely without providing any additions to the de La Tour family. Claude is said to have founded the fur trading post of Pentagouet, today's Castine, Maine, around 1613. This southernmost post to become fort in old Acadie, would precipitate considerable ire and indignation from the New Englanders and Virginians who considered this location to be part of the English land grants. It would go back and forth like a ping pong ball over the next hundred years, because it also had the strategic advantage of being the quickest way, via Indian trails and waterways, to exchange information between Acadia and New France (Quebec).

# D. Charles Turgis de Saint Étienne de La Tour vs. Charles de Menou, D'Aulnay, and Charnisay. Too Many Governors!

The King of England commands Sir William Alexander to abandon his settlement of Charlesfort, in 1631 as Acadie is once again given back to the French. In 1632 Charles de la Tour finally returns to France to obtain a delimitation between his authority and that of Cardinal Richelieu's cousin, Isaac de Razilly, a Knight in the Order of Malta, who has also received a commission as governor of Acadie. Razilly, intending to build up a colony that would eventually rival the English colonies of the south, sailed from Auray, France, with l'Esperance de Dieu and the Saint Jehan in the spring of 1632. His lieutenants were Charles de Menou, Sieur d'Aulnay and Charnisay and Nicolas Denys. He also brought over 300 "hommes d'elites", tools, livestock, seed, arms, munitions and whatever else was necessary to set up a colony at La Have. This quality effort had been achieved by Isaac, his brother, Claude and another entrepreneur by the name of Jean Condonnier pooling resources and forming the Razilly-Condonnier Company. A total of three ships were engaged in this enterprise in the beginning. Once he had repatriated 42 Scots hangers-on, for some reason he allowed a few to stay. They formed the base of the "Acadian" families whose surnames, like Melanson, sound more Scottish than French. Razilly returned to France, passing away in 1635. Although de La Tour and Razilly got along fairly well, that was not to be the case with his successors.

D'Aulnay wanted complete control but the French monarchy, thinking that there was enough to satisfy everybody, decided to divide Acadie into three areas. "D'Aulnay, who had succeeded Razilly would retain the La Have area and the Port Royal region and would have control of the area north of the Baie Francaise, (present day southern New Brunswick) except for a strip along the Saint John River which was granted to Charles de La Tour. The latter would retain a portion of the mainland of Nova Scotia and the Saint John River valley. Nicolas Denys would have control of the eastern portion of Acadia from Canso to Cap des Rosiers in Gaspe."[39] Family squabbles and discontent often begin when the patriarch divides up his lands amongst his dependants. Such a situation sprang up in Acadie, especially between La Tour and d'Aulnay. It was not only a clash of egos; it also was a clash of the manner in which each of the protagonists wanted to develop Acadia. Charles de La Tour wanted to expand the fur trade without too much infraction on the Mi'kmag who, in their benevolence, were allowing a limited colonization on their traditional lands. Charles D'Aulnay was more interested in setting up an aristocratic colonial empire on these lands and, if he had lived to old age, he might have achieved much more. His natural drive and willingness to go head to head with any who blocked his way, be they French or English, was well known to all parties. Given enough supplies, weapons and people who could and would use them, could have kept Acadia stable long enough to survive. Too many chiefs often create problems. It certainly did in this instance.

The geographic locations of these colonial fiefdoms did not correspond with the location of the power bases of these two men who managed to push Nicolas Denys to one side. D'Aulnay shifted his principal base from La Hêve to the location of present day Annapolis Royal. This was done in an effort to out maneuver de La Tour who had set up a base at Jemseg on the Saint John River. Fort Saint Louis was not totally abandoned by de La Tour, but this new bastion, more centrally located for the fur trade, was named Fort Sainte-Marie. With their power bases, including seigniorial holdings, in each others back yard, the official word from France for them to get along did not hold much water in Acadie. Both tried first to impress the other by harassing the New Englanders in the Castine area. Things really got dirty in 1639 when de La Tour captured one of d'Aulnay's ships on its way to secure Pentagouet from the English. The following year, de La Tour tried to take Port Royal with a couple of ships rented from New England merchants. D'Aulnay turned the thing around by capturing de La Tour in the act.

D'Aulnay made the mistake of letting de La Tour and his men go in a mutual prisoner exchange. "In 1642 d'Aulnay destroyed all of de La Tour's buildings at Fort St. Louis (now Villagedale, Shelburne County). In reprisal de La Tour attacked Port Royal again in the following year with the help of four armed ships from Plymouth, Mass. and one from La Rochelle, France. The fort resisted the attack, but seven of the defenders were wounded, three were killed, and de La Tour and his allies broke into the warehouses and took all the furs that were stored to a value of 18,000 pounds."[40] De La Tour collected one third of the booty and his associates received the remainder.

The reason that Charles de La Tour was so successful in his negotiations and associations with the English is that, although he had refused to become an English Baronet in his own right, he had inherited his father's title and was recognized as such. Although I am descended from the de La Tours, I must admit that they followed *Lady Luck* wherever she would bring them. Not all of their luck was good. He and his second wife, Françoise-Marie Jacqueline even pretended to be Huguenots to maintain New England goodwill. The priests and some of the soldiers left Fort La Tour for Port Royal because of this and some of them must have told d'Aulnay about Charles de La Tour heading back to Boston on a trading mission. Easter weekend, 1645 was to see Fort La Tour fall into d'Aulnay's hands.

"The defenders were led by Françoise-Marie Jacqueline. Denys says that through three days and three nights of bombardment, the Lady Commandant fought at the head of her men, surrendering only after d'Aulnay promised quarter to all and after one of her soldier's, a Swiss, accepted a bribe and let d'Aulnay's men through a breach in the wall...Casualties were heavy, and if quarter was promised, it was not given. Denys tells us that all, but one, of de La Tours men were hanged and that Françoise-Marie Jacqueline was made to watch with a rope around her neck."[41] Madame de La Tour survived the hangings but was never to leave the fort alive. June 15 is given as her date of passing but one can only speculate how this brave woman, a mother with an infant, met her fate. D'Aulnay had the *decency* to send the child back to France but it looks like he kept the boy's 2,000 pounds he would have inherited from Mm. Françoise Marie de La Tour (She had received this sum in a successful lawsuit against an English Captain in Boston). He also took the $55,000.00 worth of pelts in the fort that belonged to the father of this child.

Charles de La Tour, always the survivalist, managed to con two Puritans named Edward Gibbons and Thomas Hawkins to lend him ships and supplies to pursue a trading venture. They were going against the trend of thought in New England where the vast majority thought you should only go to war to defend the faith, not to get involved in a *Papist intrigue*.

When he found out that his wife and fort no longer existed and that d'Aulnay was *Dei Facto* ruler of Acadie, Charles *took* a ship and sailed her up to Quebec to await better times. He had lost the battle of influence in France for 1647 saw d'Aulnay was named the only Governor of Acadia. 1650 was to prove a good year for de La Tour. His rival died, probably from pneumonia, after falling out of a canoe in his own back yard. This year also saw de La Tour return to France where he convinced the King that his actions were justifiable for a man who was forced to survive under so much trial and tribulation. De La Tour returned to Acadie with both his property and his commission as governor. " At the same time, he was given official thanks for his tireless labors to convert the savages and uphold the authority of the King...It was noted too, that his pious and patriotic effort would have continued if he had not been hindered by Charles de Menou, Sieur d'Aulnay Charnisay."[42]

He even was given the financial capacity to enlist Sieur Philippe Mius d'Entremont as his second in command. Other settlers came to Acadie with them in 1651.

# Chapter 5. The Métis/Acadians Come Alive – Key Players in the First Hundred Years

## A.    Charles Amador Turgis, Sgr de La Tour, de St.-Étienne, De Sauvages, Governor and Lieutenant General of Acadia

As was mentioned earlier, Charles de Biencourt and Charles de La Tour were forced to go *underground* for a number of years as a form of self-preservation. They and their men found themselves in a primordial forest already inhabited by a substantial indigenous population who literally took them in. Many of these entrepreneurs learned the language and the ways of the Mi'kmaq and, once having accomplished that task, they combined these newly acquired skills to the skills given them by mother nature and wooed some of the First Nation women to become theirs. It is surmised that Charles de Biencourt married one of these maidens but he died in 1624 and no children have ever been mentioned.

Charles de La Tour, his successor, proved to be more successful. Around the same year that his cousin died, de La Tour married a Mi'kmaq woman (Marriage blessed 1630) who was to provide him with a number of children. His first child, a daughter, JEANNE, born in 1625, would later marry one of her father's companions, d'Apprendisteguy,

Sieur de Martignon, a Basque. They were married in Pentagouet (Castine, Maine) around 1655 and were to have children with modern descendants. Martignon raised his family in La Rochelle, France.

The second child, ANTOINETTE, born somewhere in Acadie before 1630, was sent back to France where she entered the convent. Antoinette became a nun on July 9, 1646. She was considered a famous singer, making special appearances at the Court of France.

The third child, another daughter, also born in Acadie, must not have lived very long as we have no recorded knowledge of her name although there is some indication that she may also have ended up in a convent in France. Convents were a secure haven to place girls from aristocratic backgrounds that were unable to provide an ample dowry for a wedding. In the seventeenth century, for a girl to marry well, their family had to put out substantial sums of money and/or land. In the marriage contract, these items would be enumerated and clauses were often included to safeguard the wife's rights in case of dissolution.

There is also mention of sons from a *union* of Charles de La Tour and another First Nation Woman. *Stephen* de La Tour, the name given to one of these sons, is supposed to have helped his father in the fur trade. (This information I found on the internet in a ten page article: "1593-1666 La Tour Early Settlers" by Danielle Duval LeMyre www.geocities.com/daniellla.geo).

We would be doing a disservice to Françoise-Marie Jacqueline if we do not put her family record in a more concise form. She was indeed the second wife of Charles de La Tour, a lady who put many a man to shame in the manner that she supported her husband, mentally, physically, and with such heart rarely demonstrated by any human being. Her father, Jacques, a nobleman and a physician from Nogent-le-Retrou, France, and her mother, Helene Lerminier, brought Françoise-Marie into this world around 1602 never expecting to hear of the travailles she was to undergo before her death in May, 1645. I hope that they got to enjoy some time with their Grandson (name unknown) who was born in a war zone, Jemseg, 1641, and never really got to know his Mother.

When Charles de La Tour was to wed his third wife at Port Royal on February 24, 1653, things had changed considerably. Charles had regained his Governorship of Acadia, almost two years to the day, and prior to his wedding day. He was no longer a young man, at sixty already past the normal life expectancy of those times. Jeanne de Motin, widow of Sieur Charles d'Aulnay Charnisay, was now thirty years old. She too had been through a lot from the time she set sail from France on the St. Jehan in 1636. She had born her first husband eight children (to follow) and tried to provide a stable home for a driven man during uncertain times. The financial burden that d'Aulnay, a younger son in an aristocratic society, had left her with meant that accommodation, not love, must make this third marriage work. Although Jeanne had taken a second husband that does not mean that she abandoned her d'Aulnay children. They remained in Acadia for a time before they chose to seek their fortunes back in the old country where they had important paternal links and prospects. One often wonders if a *summer* bride married to a *winter* husband can work. Looking around Southwestern Nova Scotia today where the de La Tour descendants are so numerous, something was definitely still working!

Charles himself was used to carrying a big debt load. That he owed so much to powerful members of British *high society* as well as members of French *families of means* could explain how he managed to stay in this game of high adventure for so many years. The English under Sedgewick capture much of Acadie in 1654. This includes the capture of Charles de La Tour himself. This *prisoner* is brought first to Boston, then to London, England and lo and behold, on the 9th or 10th of August1654, we find proclamations coming out of Westminster declaring that Cromwell has given the colonies of Acadia and Nova Scotia to Thomas Temple, William Crowne, and Charles de La Tour!

Cromwell's take from this was a yearly *tribute* of twenty moose hides and twenty beaver pelts. Like a modern Stock Market deal, three days later, de La Tour and Temple parlay their appointments into a deal with William Crowne that leaves him sole controller of the colonies in question. De La Tour, who still owed 3,379 Pounds, 11 Shillings to Edward Gibbons' widow (remember the boat he had *borrowed* to flee to Quebec with), had this sum repaid on his behalf. He not only was allowed to take up residence once again in Acadia, he was to receive an annual payment equal to 20% of all profits realized from the colonies whether it be from the fur trade, agriculture, or mining. When Charles died sometime in 1663, he certainly could have had no regrets for having lived a boring life!

The children of Charles St. Étienne de La Tour and Jeanne Motin de Reux, born Circa 1615 in Charolais, France, daughter of Louis Motin, Sieur de Reux de Courcelles Died circa 1670 in Acadia, include:

1.  Marie-Born @ 1654 in Jemseg; Died 30 May1739, Port Royal, Acadie. Marie married, 1674, Alexandre LeBorgne, Sieur de Belisle, Governor of Acadie. This couple had children with modern descendants.

2.  Jacques- Born @ 1655 at River St.Jean, Acadie. Died in Port Royal, Acadie before the 1698 census. Jacques married Anne Melanson, 1685. This couple had children with modern descendants.

3.  Marguerite – Born @ 1658 at River St.Jean, Acadie. Died in Pobumcoup, Acadie, 16 July1748. Marguerite first wed @ 1676, Abraham Mius de Pleinmarais. This couple had children with modern descendants. Abraham died before, 5 September1704. Marguerite remarried, 27 June1705, Jean-Francois Villate.

4.  Anne – Born @ 1661 River St.Jean, Acadie. Died in Pobumcoup, Acadie, after 15 September1738, Anne married, 1678, Jacques Mius d'Entremont de Pobumcoup. This couple had children with modern descendants.

4a. Their son, Philippe Mius d'Entremont married THERESE de St-Castin, daughter of Jean-Vincent d'Abbadie de St.-Castin, and Marie Madokawando, daughter of a great Abanaki Chief.

* Bona Arsenault has written letters that the ARCEMENT families of Isle-St.-Jean (Prince Edward Island) are their descendants via Jacques and Anne's son, Pierre Claude d'Entremont married to Marie Josephe Terriot.

5. Charles – Born before 2 March1663. Died in Louisbourg, Isle Royale (Cape Breton), 11 August1731. Charles married Jeanne-Angelique Loreau (Laureau), @1688. All of his adult life, Charles was involved with the military defense of his homeland. As a soldier he was wounded at the fall of Port Royal in 1710.He was made Chevalier St-Louis in 1728.

*Have we given a complete list of the progeny of Charles de La Tour, I am not certain. Did he have other children with First Nation women? The possibility exists but the records do not. There will always be an air of uncertainty with regards to this issue, whether it is Charles de La Tour, or some of the other men we are about to look at. In many cases, we will not be looking at *complete* family histories as we just did with this family. One of the main purposes of this book is to follow the aboriginal blood as it pertains to the Métis/Acadians of our community – past and present.

# B. The d'Abbadie de Saint-Castins of Old Acadie, the Métis Connection

When dealing with the de La Tours, it was mentioned that one of Charles' grandsons, we'll call him Philippe Mius d'Entremont III, married into the Saint-Castin family. He actually married a daughter of Jean-Vincent d'Abbadie, 3rd Baron of Saint-Castin and his second wife, Marie around 1685. The Baron's first wife, Mathilde, was her sister, an older daughter of Madokawando, Chief of the Abanaki's in the Penobscot, Maine, U.S.A. section of Old Acadie whom he had married not long after arriving there in 1670 with Governor Grandfontaine. [43]

Children from this first marriage are as follows:

1. CLAIRE, Born @ 1671, she married @ 1700 Paul Meunier, son of Jean and Marguerite Housseau. Claire died between 27/28 December 1744. They had children with modern descendants.

2. Unnamed DAUGHTER, who married @ 1695 a Monsieur Meneux called Chateauneuf. She and her children were captured and brought to Boston in 1704.

3. Another unnamed DAUGHTER, who married Philippe Meunier, Paul's brother, sometime before 1703.

4. ANASTASIE, married on 4th of December 1707, Alexandre Le Borgne de Belisle, son of Alexandre Le Borgne and Marie de Saint-Étienne de La Tour. This would comprise one of the Métis/Acadian roots of the Le Borgne family.

5. BERNARD, born around 1688, this young man entered the Seminary in Quebec on 22 October1696. His life was short lived as he drowned on the way to France on 24 November1704.

6. BERNARD-ANSELME, born @ 1689. He married Charlotte D'Amours de Chauffours, daughter of Louis D'Amours and Marguerite Guyon. According to historian Robert LeBlant, Bernard-Anselme died in Bearn, France, in the fall of 1720.

7. JEAN- PIERRE, born @ 1692, entered the Seminary in Quebec on 30 July 1701. Here we have another young man who was never to achieve his potential as he passed away on 17 December1702 at the tender age of 12.

8. URSULINE, born @ 1696. She married @ 1715 Louis D'Amours de     Chauffours, Son of Mathieu D'Amours and Louise Guyon. In 1767 Ursuline is recorded in the Census of Miquelon Island, France, off the eastern coast of Canada. She died 18 January1768 at l'Hopital de St-Pol-de-Leon.

9. JOSEPH (d'Abbadie) married, after 1728, an unidentified female. He died after March 1751.

10. BARENOS (De Saint-Castin) married @ 1725 an unidentified female. Barenos died on 25 August1746. The cause of death, given in a letter sent by Beauharnois to the French Ministry dated 4 October1746, was two fatal blows with a knife that was doled out to him by one of his *sauvage* nephews.[44]

As you can see, not all of the females, neither Amerindian nor European, can be successfully identified. If you are interested in researching the St-Castins (with their many derivatives), the D'Amours (obviously ancestors of Louis D'Amours, prolific American author who wrote numerous novels about the American west as well as many other stories of action and intrigue), or the Meuniers, or the Le Bourgnes de Belisle, you now have somewhere to start. Related ancestors and families to Saint-Castin include: Guyon, Dion, Marsolet, Marsolais, D'Amours, d'Abbadie, Mius, Meunier, Lemire , Labbadie, Morpain, Le Borgne, Lemyre, Motin, Latour, Housseau, Doucette, Comeau, Saillant, Paradis, Leblanc, Roy, Reyau, Lavielle, Nicolau, Coulomme, Robardie, Boudreau, Abadie, Sarthopon, Pierre de Bourbon, Dufau de Lalongue, Robdais, and Martin.

# B. The Denys of Acadie, an Important Family That Was Hard to Hate!-

When Issac de Razilly first came to Acadie in 1632, he had brought two *second in commands,* his cousin, Charles de Menou d'Aulnay, and Nicolas Denys, son and grandson of provincial officers in Tours, France. Razilly was the boss and he got along well enough with Charles de La Tour. They seemed to see themselves as the same but different. De La Tour still had his prior territorial rights while Razilly was a creation of Cardinal de Richelieu. Everything changed after Razilly's sudden death in La Hêve on 2nd July1636. Denys was in charge of developing the fisheries, the lumber trade and, of course, the lucrative fur trade. D'Aulnay, being the military man, was in charge of enforcing the Treaty of St. Germain en Laye which, in March of 1632 had given Acadie back to France. This meant clearing out the Scots and repatriating them to their native soil. Razilly's death meant to d'Aulnay that he was now in charge.

I'm certain that the thought that *Might is Right* came to mind to M. de Menou, considering that he held the largest military force in the colony. De La Tour still had his supporters in France, as did Nicolas Denys. We will restate the royal division cooked up in the Mother Country. "D'Aulnay...would retain the La Have area and the Port Royal region and would have control of the area north of the Baie Francaise, (present day southern New Brunswick) except a strip along the Saint John River which was granted to Charles de La Tour. The latter would retain a portion of the mainland of Nova Scotia and the Saint John River valley. Nicolas Denys would have control of the eastern portion of Acadia from Canso to Cap des Rosiers in Gaspe."[45] At a time when the struggling colony required some stability, the decision makers were almost waving a red flag at the English colonies to the south.  The larger colony of Quebec had lost its patriarch, Samuel de Champlain, a mere six months before.

Nicolas Denys tried to establish fishing stations at Port Rossignol (Brooklyn, Queen's County), at Miscou (1645) and fortifications at St. Peters and St. Anne's in Cape Breton. His brother, Simon, was assisting him in Cape Breton. D'Aulnay's widow, Jeanne Motin, trying to maintain some kind of financial control over the region, had them whisked off to Quebec as prisoners in 1651. With eight children to look out for and creditors knocking on her door (d'Aulnay would have sunk in debt if the canoe had not got him first) The Le Borgnes were looking for their pound of flesh. They even badgered the Denys brothers in 1652 when they tried to set up a post at Nipisiguit (Bathurst), taking them as prisoners to Port Royal.

After 1657 the Le Bourgnes de Belisle were to become the power brokers in Acadie yet Nicolas received his piece of the pie on 30th January1654 when his royal commission arrived. It gave him seigniorial ownership rights over Cape Breton, Isle St-Jean, and the surrounding smaller islands.[46] It is difficult to hate a person who keeps coming and coming no matter what you throw at him. Not only is Nicolas Denys known as a survivor. This man who lived a full life left us with written documentation of an era when most of the protagonists preferred to fight with the sword rather than the pen!

I would be remiss in my duties as an author not to follow the above mentioned remark with a quote from Nicolas Denys' book (Description geographique des cotes de l'Amerique Septentriolane) describing the landscape surrounding Port Royal while he was held prisoner there in 1653. Denys' states: "There are numbers of meadows on both shores, and two islands which possess meadows, and which are 3 or 4 leagues from the fort in ascending. There is a great extent of meadows which the sea used to cover, and which the Sieur d'Aulnay had drained. It bears now fine and good wheat, and since the English have been masters of the country, the residents who were lodged near the fort have for the most part abandoned their houses and have gone to settle on the upper part of the river. They have made their clearings below and above the great meadow, which belongs at present to Madame de La Tour. There they have again drained other lands which bear wheat in much greater abundance than those which they cultivated around the fort, good though those were. All the inhabitants there are the ones whom Monsieur le Commandeur de Razilly had brought from France to La Have; since that time they have multiplied much at Port Royal, where they have a great number of cattle and swine"[47]

Obviously he was trying to entice people to settle in Acadia shortly after he himself had retired from its coasts to return to France in 1670. The last straw for Nicolas probably was the burning down of his trading post at St. Peters by Sieur de La Giraudiere in 1668. When you are burnt out of house and home, unable to save any of the contents, after so many years of trying, it would take the wind out of anybody's sail. He had spent almost forty years in Acadia trying to develop the colony. If he had been more successful at bringing in new *recruits* to colonize his enterprises, his business ventures might have born more fruit. While in Acadia, Denys maintained excellent relations with the First Nations. One of his sons was to take this relationship to the next level.

Nicolas Denys, son of Jacques Denys, Sieur Du Pressoir, and Marie Cosnier daughter of the King's chamberlain, born at Tours, France, 2nd June1603.Nicolas married 1st October1642, Marguerite de Lafitte, daughter of Pierre Lafitte, a bourgeois merchant, from Bordeaux .Nicolas died in France in 1688.This couple had seven children but we will only be examining two for our purposes.

1.  Marie married @ 1666 Michel Le Neuf de La Valliere from Quebec. His career in Canada spans from becoming Seigneur of Beaubassin (one of our ancient communities), 24 October1676 to Governor of Acadia 1683/84. Marie died before the 1st July1687.

2.  Richard (de Fronsac), born in La Rochelle 29 August1647. Richard married @ 1680

Anne Patarabego, a member of the First Nations. This son took over the family business from his father after years of learning the business. "During the winter of 1668-1669, a fire destroyed the buildings and business Richard and his father had established in St. Peters, in Cape Breton. They then moved to Nipisiguit (Bathurst). In the fall of 1691, Richard Denys died at sea. The ship on which he had embarked for Quebec, Le Saint-Francois-Xavier, was lost with all hands."[48]

The children of Richard Denys, Sieur de Fronsac and Seigneur of Miramichi, and his first wife, Anne Patarabego, include:

1.  MARIE-ANNE born January 1681. She married on 16th October1709, Jean Mercan, called Lapierre Marie-Anne died at Pointe Aux Trembles de Montreal on 9th October1728.

2.  NICOLAS (dit Fronsac), born @ 1682. Like his father, he also married a First Nation woman, Marie. Nicolas died on the 3rd February1732. This couple had at least four children: Marie born @ 1702, married @ 1725 Michel Masson. She died on 4/5 August 1732. Francois born @ 1708, died 22 January1732. Gabriel born @ 1716, died 28 December1732. Jacques born @ 1717, died 6th February1732. When you look at the staggered deaths of these siblings throughout 1732, one must conclude that one of the pestilences of that age must be the cause. More time and research than this author has available will tell the complete story of the Métis/Acadian Denys of our ancestral home.

The Michau, a Mi'kmag family that moved to Cape Breton sometime after 1713, may provide a key to heretofore unexplored by genealogists. The grandchildren of Jean Michau, the first of the Michaux of Cape Breton, received special attention from the French in Louisbourg. These sons of Michel Michau and Marie Isodore were both baptized in the parish church there. That, in itself, is not an astounding fact although Mi'kmag children were not often accorded this *honor*. Who their Godparents were is what was out of the ordinary. Jacques Ange, baptized 17 August1729, had Réné Lambert Desgranges, artillery officer, and Marie Courtiau, wife of the King's prosecutor. Francois, baptized 28 October1734, had for Godparents Joseph Duvivier, artillery officer, and Dame Angelique Laureau de La Tour, widow of a former captain in the garrison. A closer scrutiny of family connections before the Michaux left mainland Acadia could solve this puzzle.

One must not forget the family and descendants of Simon Denys, Sieur de la Trinite, elder brother of Nicolas Denys the Elder. Partnering with his brother in the days of Razilly, Simon cut quite a swath in his own right, having seven children by his first wife, Jeanne Dubreuil, and according to Stephen White, fifteen with his second wife, Françoise Dutertre. Such a virulent and robust person set loose amongst his friends, the Mi'kmag may well have left some Métis children on the coasts of Acadie. Lots of his children could have done the same.

# D. Charles de Menou Sieur d'Aulnay de Charnisay Governor of Acadia -by Right or Might?

We have well documented the fact that d'Aulnay had brought over Jeanne Motin to become his lawful wedded wife in 1638. We established that between them they were to have eight children, four boys and four girls, between their wedding date and M. d'Aulnay's death on 24ᵗʰ May1650. All for of their sons: Joseph; Charles; Réné; and Paul were destined to fall on the battlefields of France. Three of their daughters: Renée; Jeanne; and Anne were destined where noble girls without a suitable dowry ended up, in the religious life where they remained until God called them back to Him. This left only the eldest daughter of this union to make any claims on the d'Aulnay Estates. Marie born @ 1639 found herself contested for this inheritance by her de La Tour half brothers and sisters when the time came. This only surviving member of the d'Aulnay – Motin alliance died in Poussay, France in 1693

Although the records show that d'Aulnay was only married once, that does not leave out the presumption that he had other liaisons that resulted in other children. One name that does come up from just such a liaison with a First Nation woman is a son, known as *Dony*. Had his father lived and continued his grasp at empire, I'm certain that we would have heard much more about this young man. Without a doubt, d'Aulnay had been stabilizing has colony and flexing his military might to such an extent that he was being given serious consideration by the Puritans of New England. In 1650 there were 45 to 50 families, living in the Port Royal La Have area under his care. These people, along with the people involved with Charles de La Tour and Nicolas Denys would form the nucleus of the families destined to be known as Acadians.

Wherever possible, especially in the Bay of Fundy area where we have the world's highest tidal ranges, d'Aulnay brought in settlers from Aunis, Saintonge, and other parts of France to set up a land reclamation system that would become almost synonymous with the Acadians themselves – the aboiteaux or dyke system. Rather than going through the tedious and time consuming method of cutting, uprooting, and clearing out virgin forests to provide themselves with arable land, they drained the salt marshes through a combination of tidal draining and dykes fitted with *flapper valve* gates that would let the salt water out and prevent it from coming back in. This took a fraction of the time and effort to prepare soil the old fashioned way and the soil, once enough rain water had desalinated it enough, proved to be of an excellent quality. Provided with time to hunt, fish, trap, and spend some quality time with their families, it is from this time on that the Acadian identity begins to develop.

King Louis XIV replaced his worn out father, Louis XIII, in 1643 at the age of five. "In 1650, when d'Aulnay died, the Sun King was still a little boy. Affairs of state were in the hands of Richelieu's successor, Cardinal Mazarin, and the mother, Queen Anne of Austria. She was said to be in love with the cardinal. The bourgeoisie and nobility were not, and between 1648 and 1653 they launched successive, unsuccessful rebellions, collectively called the Fronde."[49] Could one of the reasons have been a question as to who really was the new King's real father. Young Louis had popped up after 23 years of marriage. Perhaps the Queen had put more men on the job? Irregardless of the reason, this left Acadia without strong leadership from the Mother country when it needed it.

Historian Rameau de Saint Père, drawing from accounts by an early priest of the colony, Ignace de Senlis, Tells us: " On Sunday, the Acadian farmers emerged from the folds of this charming valley, some in canoes, others on horseback, their wives and daughters riding behind, while long lines of Micmac, brightly painted and with colorful ornaments, mingled with them. Around the church grounds, d'Aulnay had developed extensive green areas, in which were called les champs commune, where the arrivals tethered their mounts and left their belongings. After the service, the colonists relaxed on the champs commune, discussing crops, hunting, progress of clearing the land, the work undertaken by the Seigneur, a thousand and one topics about their private lives and gossiping the way it is done in all the French countries."[50] The Acadians were left to themselves, especially now that the intrigues associated with the English Civil War between the followers of King Charles I were pitted in a losing cause against the *will* of Parliament, championed by Oliver Cromwell.

# E. Germain Doucet, Sieur de La Verdure - Major (Captain-at-Arms) Father of one of the Great Métis/ Acadian Families

A native of Couperans-in-Brie, in France, Germain was born @1595. He first arrived in Acadia as a soldier with Razilly and d'Aulnay in 1632. La Verdure, as we shall call this gentleman to differentiate between him and his many descendants of the same name, became d'Aulnay's right hand man when this worthy person became Governor of Acadia. On the 14th July1640, La Verdure made a formal appearance in Port Royal, alongside Issac Pesseley and Guillaume Trahan, at an inquiry convened to dispute the legitimacy of Charles de Saint Étienne de La Tour's dealings in Acadia, specifically the naval action that had taken place between the two Governors earlier that year. His role then was as *Master-at-Arms* at Pentagouet. When he was not playing a military role, La Verdure was in charge of the proper instruction of his benefactor's children. He even was an executer of d'Aulnay's will at the time of his demise. This came to be because d'Aulnay's father, Renée, who had been named guardian of his grandchildren, had not gone to collect these unfortunates himself. The man whom he had sent, Sieur de Saint Mars proved unacceptable to the widow, their mother. She asked and received proper assistance from her husband's right hand man and closest friend, Germain Doucet. Furthermore, it was La Verdure who personally escorted his friend's eight children back to France. He then returned to Port Royal to reassume his posting as Master-at-Arms of the capitol, a post that he had assumed in 1645 after the demise of Issac Pessley.

Sieur Charles de Menou d'Aulnay's feelings towards M. Doucet is made very apparent in the recommendations that he made to the Capuchin Monk, Father Pascal, intended for his father, Renée. "Some debts I have of little consequence, and for my soul, for the which I have received my needs, I want to give Germain Doucet dit La Verdure, of the parish of Couperan-en-Brie, cinquante escus of income for the rest of his life and that of his wife's, in recognition for the love he has always shown towards me." http://www.shocking.com/~gregbard/geneology/not06533.shtml Page 4

La Verdure seems to be another of those pragmatists who made the best of the situation, whatever came his way. He signed as witness to the marriage of his best friend's widow, Jeanne de Motin, and his best friend's enemy, Charles de Saint-Étienne de La Tour. That these two men could put things behind them is made very apparent by the fact that Germain Doucet retains his position in charge of Port Royal until Major Robert Sedgewick with his three warships and 500 men came knocking at his door on the 1st of August, 1654. This was less than two weeks after he had crushed de La Tour's other forts including Fort Saint-Jean where de La Tour himself had been captured and relieved of over 10,000 gold Louis (Louis= 10 Pounds, 24 pence). Cromwell's *reign* in England from the time of King Charles I's decapitation until his death in 1658 (followed in 1660 by the restoration of the monarchy under Charles II) was not in the best interest of Acadia. These attacks took place when England and France were not even supposed to be at war.

The siege lasted sixteen days when La Verdure, hopelessly outnumbered by almost five to one, capitulated. The terms of surrender between Mr. La Verdure and Mr. Robert Sedgewick are worth noting. "The Sieur came out of the Fort with his garrison with their weapons and beating drums, flag deployed, **balle en bouche,** musket or gun on shoulders, wick burning on both ends, and their baggage. They will be granted safe passage to France with their provisions for two months. As for the children (of d'Aulnay) we will take possession of all the furniture, property, merchandise and animals that belong to them. The inhabitants will have freedom of conscience, and can live in their own homes and property with all the furniture that belongs to them. Their staying by means of recognition of their Seigneurial duty for which they are obliged to pay by their grants; with the freedom to sell said furniture and property as seemeth good to English persons or the French who are staying in the Country... and to ensure the above articles are followed, The Sieur La Verdure has left as hostage Mr. Jacques Bourgeois, his brother-in –law and Lieutenant of the area, and the Sieur Emmanuel Le Borgne, son, until the terms of the treaty have been fulfilled. We have signed, Robert Bourgeois, Robert Sedgewick, Robert Salem, Marke Harrison, Robert Martin, Richard Morse, plus the Reverend Father Leonard de Chartres and Mr. Guillaume Trouen (Trahan), representative of the people and the Sieur Borgne (Father)" http:// www.shocking.com/~gregbard P. 5/6

The English, although at the time of these attacks and sacks were not at war with France maintained nominal control of Acadia until 1670. Germain Doucet, his last wife and those of the garrison who wished to do so, returned to France, there to stay. Surprisingly, his sons and daughters remained in Acadia. They were to become important building blocks of the Acadian and Métis/Acadian identities in the upcoming years. We now begin their story.

There is some difficulty in ascertaining who the wife, or wives, of Germain Doucet, Sieur de La Verdure, born @ 1595 in Couperans en Brie, France were. Some state that he came from France with his first wife Marie Bourgeois, sister of a fellow military man Jacques Bourgeois who also came to Acadia with Razilly in 1632. They further state that this Jacques had two nephews, Robert, another military man, and Jacob also known as Jacques, who was a military surgeon. This would make sense with the above mentioned quote and Stephen White's contention that Germain the elder could not be married to the sister of Jacques Bourgeois, the nephew, who was a much younger man.

This does not leave any doubt about the fact that the young Bourgeois and Jeanne Trahan are the originators of the Bourgeois family line in Acadia especially since the other two Bourgeois males returned to France with Germain in 1654.

Although Germain Doucet, Major, Captain-at-Arms, is buried somewhere in France, his bloodlines, both Métis/Acadian and Acadian run very deep in Acadia and other parts of the world, both Old and New, to this day. His first marriage took place some time prior to 1620 in France. The children of this marriage were the following:

1. Pierre born @ 1621, died June1713. He married @1660, Henriette Pelletret born circa 1641, died before the census of 1693, daughter of Simon and Pérrine Bourg.

2. Louise Marguerite born @1625, died 19/20 December1707. She married @1647 Abraham Dugas, born 1618 in Toulouse, Languedoc, France. A gunsmith and good friend of her father who had also come to Acadia with Razilly.

3. Unnamed DAUGHTER, who, according to Stephen White, married Pierre Le Jeune Jr., aka. Briard, @1650 at Port Royal.

We now come upon another Germain Doucet, born circa 1641, died circa 1696 Port Royal, who is to wed, @1664, Marie Landry (Réné and Pérrine Bourg). According to a declaration made by this Germain's

Great-Great Grandson in Belle-Ile-En-Mer, France when they were trying to reconstitute the lost or burnt records that fell victim to the Deportation and its aftermath, this ancestor came from Canada (New France).

Why would this Pierre Doucet want to discount any association with the first Germain Doucet who, by all recorded events, carried himself as a man of trust and honor? Certainly the sire could not be the problem. Could it have been the dame?

It cannot be beyond all reasonable doubt that La Verdure may have fathered this child with an aboriginal maiden at a time in his life when so many of his companions, finding themselves alone, took native women as wives or long term lovers? This would coincide with the conclusion made by Stephen White as follows: "The dispensation for the third to the fourth degree of kindred granted upon the marriage of Pierre Doucet, grandson of Germain Doucet (2) and Marie Laundry, to Anne-Marie Dugas, great-granddaughter of Abraham Dugas and Marguerite Doucet (Rg Port Royal 27 Jan 1749), makes it certain that Germain and Marguerite were brother and sister."[51] This would make Germain Doucet Jr. the progenitor of many of the Métis/Acadian people of Acadia. The constant intermarriage of Acadian families sees their blood intermingle with other families, and as the abovementioned case indicates, at times this blood received and *infusion* of the same family blending again and again. In certain families like the Doucets, this happens on many occasions. The children of this Germain and Marie Landry are as follows:

a.  Charles born @1665, died 7/8 May1739. Married @ 1684 Huguette Guerin (Francois & Anne Blanchard). Their sixth child, Germain (3) born circa 1697, bears mentioning. His first wife was Françoise Comeau (Alexandre & Marguerite Doucet) whom he married in Port Royal on 26 November1726. His second wife whom he married in Beaubassin on 30 October1741 was of Mi'kmag descent. Her name was Françoise Sauvage (Thomas & Anne Lapierre).

b.  Bernard called La Verdure, born circa 1667, died in Port Royal 4 August1709. He married @1690 Madeleine Corporon (Jean & Françoise Savoie)

c.  Laurent born @1669, died before19 January1728.Bernard married @ 1689 Jeanne Babin (Antoine & Marie Mercier)

d.  Jacques called Maillard, born @1671. He married circa 1695, Marie Pellerin (Étienne & Jeanne Savoie)

e.  Claude called Maitre Jean, born @1674, died in Port Royal 5/6 December 1754. Married @ 1696 Marie Comeau (Étienne & Marie-Anne Lefebvre)

f.  Marie born @1678

g.  Jeanne born @1680, died before 7 January1733. She married @1702 Jean-Chrysostome Loppinot

h.  Alexis born @1682

i.  Pierre born @1685

# F. Philippe Mius d'Entremont, Sieur de Pobomcoup – Major-at-Arms, King's Attorney 1670-1688 Ancestor to one of the Most Prolific Métis/Acadian Families in Existence

Whenever one wants to begin an animated conversation about Métis and/or Acadian families in Acadia, especially in the Cape Sable region, all you have to do is bring out the difference between being a Muise (Mius) or a d'Entremont. The truth is self evident in their common ancestor's name and has been commented upon earlier. All Muises are Muises and all d'Entremonts are Muises. The distinction between the two branches of the same family supposedly was entrenched around the Muise branch being primarily the issue of mixed blood, Mi'kmag and Acadian, while those who were of pure Acadian stock would wear the name d'Entremont. This division was instigated by Benoni, great grandson of Philippe (1), who dropped the Mius and retained the name d'Entremont as his given surname. Joseph, Philippe's grandson (also called d'Azy), dropped the d'Entremont and kept the original Mius as his family name. There has been a stigma attached to this rupture that carries on to this very day. This book is set for publication as part of the 2004 Congres Mondiale celebration in Nova Scotia. What a missed opportunity to reunite this family in an atmosphere of levity and nostalgia rather than having two separate events that celebrate their difference rather than their uniqueness.

Philippe Mius, Sieur d'Entremont, Seigneur de Pobomcoup, was born in Normandy in 1609. He arrived in Acadia with Charles de La Tour in 1651, retained as his Major-General. On 17 July1653, Charles rewarded Philippe and Pierre Ferrand ( Mr. Ferrand is listed in the *letters patent* received from Governor de La Tour but that is all we hear about him) with a fiefdom in the Cape Sable region on the east side of Pubnico Harbor. This seigneury, known as *la Baronnie de Pobomcoup,* supposedly measured one mile of coastline going inland four miles. According to Père Clarence d'Entremont, Philippe d'Entremont and his family were vandalized and robbed by a privateering force in the employ of the Dutch in 1675, who for a brief period of time considered Acadia theirs under the name of New Holland. Sieur d'Entremont had made quite an improvement on this property to such an extent that, in the 1671 census of Pobomcoup, he was said to be in possession of 29 horned animals, 29 sheep, 12 goats, 20 pigs, and over six acres of cleared land. He also had with him at this time the two sons of his former benefactor, Sieur de La Tour.

These *corsairs* had already wrecked havoc on Pentagouet the summer before making prisoners of Grandfontaine's successor as governor, Jacques de Chambly, and Vincent de Saint-Castin. This had been followed up by the capturing of a number of Acadian outposts while heading towards the St. John River where they intended to make war on the fort at Jemseg under the command of Pierre de Joybert, Seigneur de Soulanges and de Marson. He had received reinforcement from Port Royal so they backed down and sailed to Boston, a friendly port now that their countryman, William of Orange, was on the English throne. Governor Frontenac of New France protested strongly to Governor Leverett of Massachusetts because at this time their countries were not at war! The following summer they took on a number of New Englanders including John Laverdure*, son of Pierre Laverdure/Melanson and Priscilla. This couples other sons included *adopted* Acadians Pierre and Charles Melanson who would become the ancestors of this very Acadian family of today.

This group, commanded by Peter Rodrigo, strong-armed the captain of the vessel *Edward and Thomas,* a Thomas Mitchell into joining the enterprise and act as navigator for the small fleet, up the Bay of Fundy as far as Siccanecto (Chignecto). They stopped in the Bay of Casco (where they took four sheep), then on to Pemaquid, to Knoskeet (Penobscot), to Muspeka Racke (Jonesport), to Maylichyous (Machias) to attack the fortress at Jemseg, on the St. John River. Once again this position was too strongly defended so they decided to make for easier pickings on the other side of the Bay of Fundy in Cape Sable. They made the Tusket River island chain and then proceeded to anchor in Pubnico Harbor, called Twelve Penny Harbor by the New Englanders. Here they pillaged the *Lantrimony* (d'Entremont) family taking what they wanted and killing their animals. John Thomas, one of these corsairs, fired shot at one of the occupants, presumably Philippe d'Entremont himself.[52] This could be why the Baron decided to bring his family with him where-ever he served in his capacity as Prosecutor-General of the King in Acadia.

In 1678 we find Philippe Mius d'Entremont and his family at Port Royal. The following year they set up house in Beaubassin where the new Governor, Michel le Neuf, Sieur de la Valliere, has his seat. They return to Port Royal in 1684, the residence of the new Governor, Francois-Marie Perrot. Governor Perrot is replaced by Sieur Louis- Alexandre des Friches de Meneval in 1687. Philippe resigned his position not long afterwards and most likely spent his retirement years at Grand-Pré at the home of his daughter, Marguerite Melanson. The Baron died around the year 1700, having contributed much mentally, physically and biologically to this young colony. His wife, Madeleine is thought to have passed away some twenty-five years earlier.

What happened to the Baronnie? Philippe Mius d'Entremont (2) had remained in La Have where he had married a Mi'kmag maiden and set up residence there. Abraham Mius d'Entremont founded his own settlement with his bride Marguerite de St.-Étienne de La Tour at Port-Razoir, near present day Shelburne.

This left Jacques Mius d'Entremont and his wife, Anne St-Étienne de La Tour, to occupy the Pubnico grant, which he did. This family was to be one of the first to be deported in 1755 but it was also one of the first to return after the hostilities had ceased. They were the only family of Acadians fortunate enough to return to their original area although the majority of them established homes on the western side of Pubnico Harbor.

*I wish to make note at this time that this same John Laverdure had a primary role to play in the capturing and bringing into slavery a number of Abanaki from Machias and a number of Mi'kmaq from Cape Sable. John, who knew their language, enticed them aboard the ship *Endeavor*. John Horton was the Captain of this 1675/76 expedition but the man in charge was Henry Lawton. Sources vary as to actual numbers taken but consensus states nine from Machias and seventeen from Cape Sable including, according to Père Clarence d'Entremont, a Sagamore and his wife. The human cargo was destined for the Azores to be sold to the Spaniards. This would spark Native uprisings against the New Englanders creating much fear and hatred amongst these settlers, a fear that would not be alleviated until the Natives and their friends were purged from the Acadian frontier. These slave traders were brought to *justice* in Boston but the only person who really lost anything was John Laverdure's mother, Priscilla, who put up a 100 Pound bond for her son who absconded and left the bond forfit.53

Recapping the stats for Philippe Mius d'Entremont, Baron de Pobumcoup Born 1609 in Normandy, died 1700 in Grand Pré, Acadia. He married @ 1649 Madeleine Helie, another person from Normandy. Madeleine was born @1626 and died before the census of 1678. Their children were:

1. Marguerite born @1650 in France, died after the census of 1714 at St-Charles-des-Mines, Acadia. Marguerite married @1665 Pierre Melanson (Pierre & Priscilla...) called Laverdure born circa 1632. Pierre was a Captain of Militia in the Minas Basin area and died in the same location as his wife before the 1714 census. This couple had ten children who were to form one of the two branches of the Melanson family in Acadia.

2. Jacques (1), Sieur de Pobomcoup, was born in Acadia @ 1654, died according to Père C. d'Entremont between the 17th July1735 and 28 June1736. Jacques married @1678 Anne de St.-Étienne de La Tour (Charles & Jeanne Motin de Reux). Anne born @ 1661 died 15 September1738. Their descendants populated the Pubnico area before the Expulsion or married well into the Acadian/French *aristocracy* before the French dream of empire came to an end in 1761/63.

3. Abraham, Sieur de Plienmaris (Plemarch) born in Acadia @1658, died before 5 September1704. In 1679, Abraham married Marguerite de St.-Étienne de La Tour (Charles & Jeanne de Motin de Reux). Marguerite born 1660. This couple had nine children but the majority of them either did not survive childhood or left very few progeny. The exception to this trend, however, may not have carried on the family name, but many of her descendants are amongst us to this day, either in this province or the Acadian *satellites*.

*The baby of a family of nine, Marie-Josephte born circa 1698 died, 29 June 1770 in Cherbourg, France. 14 October1717 Marie-Josephe married Réné Landry (Pierre Landry & Madeleine Robichaud). Their families, along with 151 other souls, were deported from Cape Sable to England ending up in France around 1760. Réné did not survive the Atlantic crossing.

Their eldest daughter, also named Marie-Josephte born 1718, married Charles d'Entremont (Charles d'Entremont & Marguerite Landry). In 1767 they were in Cherbourg with two children.

Her brother, Joseph Landry born 1721, married twice, first to Cécile d'Entremont (Joseph & Cécile Boudreau) who died before 1763, and secondly to Jeanne Marie Varangue (Antoine Varangue & Jeanne Terrier.

Their sister, Marguerite born 1730 married Jacques d'Entremont (Joseph & Cécile Boudreau). Another sister, Anne born 1736 married Jean Granger (Pierre & Anne Belliveau). I have added these grandchildren of Abraham Mius d'Entremont and Marguerite de La Tour simply to provide a link to those Acadians/Cajuns from the other areas who may be descended from this couple.

4. Philippe (2) d'Azy born in Acadia @1660. This Philippe was to initiate a Mius d'Entremont strain that combined him with two Mi'kmag wives, producing the most prolific Métis/Acadian population of the whole Acadian era past and present! The name of his first wife is not handed down to us. Their *union* initiated @1678 and lasted until her death in the mid 1680's

A. Joseph d'Azy born @1679 died Port Royal 13/14 December1729. Joseph married @1699 Marie Amireau called *Tourangeau* (Francois & Marie Pitre)

B. Marie born circa 1680 married @1697 Francois Viger (Francois & ...)

C. Maurice born a twin @1682 married circa 1702 a Mi'kmag maiden named Marguerite.

D. Mathieu other twin born circa 1682 married @1706 a Mi'kmag maiden named Marie-Madeleine.

E. Françoise born before 1687 married Jacques Bonnevie called *Beaumont*. According to Stephen White, it appears that Françoise, her husband, and her family, were among the unfortunates who set sail in an English transport out of Ile St-Jean in 1758 only to perish at sea.

*m 2 circa 1687 Marie* born @1670 Mi'kmag maiden

F. Jacques born @1688 married circa 1715 an unknown woman most likely from the Mi'kmag Nation.. He was with his father and associates on the sea raid, mentioned in the notes about his sister, Madeleine's, family (Look down to (I).

G. Marie born @1690 married to Jean-Baptiste Thoma (Thomas) born at Port Royal @1680. This man may have been called Thomas Albiston, or Albistou, on the French census of 1708 and 1722. He may be of English and Mi'kmag descent. In 1726 he is the head chief at Port Royal, with Jacques Noucout, who may be the son of old Captain Jacques Noucout. He is probably the Thoma who took over a sloop at Minas in 1737 with the Noucouts and Bartholomew Anquarret and was the one who spoke on behalf of the Cape Sable Mi'kmag in 1753. Jean-Baptiste was probably the Thoma at Ponhook in 1758 due to his close association with the Muis, the Guidry (Labrador), and the Le Jeune families. He always remained faithful to the Catholic religion and seems to have known Maillard before 1762. This grand old man was wooed by Thomas Wood on behalf of the British and the Anglican Church from 1762 to 1768 when he went to have his son Joseph baptized by Father Bailey at Piziquid (Windsor).

H. Pierre, also called d'Azy, born @ 1691 married @1718 Marguerite LaPierre (Francois called Laroche & Jeanne Rimbault) born 1693.In 1753, Pierre Mieuius was considered the chief of a First Nation camp at River St-Jean.

I. Madeleine also called d'Azy, born @1694 married before 1708 Jean-Baptiste Guedry (Claude & Marguerite Petitpas). This lady was destined to lose both husband and son in an adventure gone wrong. Her father had them embroiled in what became known as an act of piracy off Merliguesh (Lunenburg, N.S.) in September 1726. Samuel Daly had them prosecuted in Boston along with three Mi'kmag. They were all found guilty and hanged on 13 November1726.[54]

J. Jean-Baptiste born @ 1696 married @ 1720 Marie of the Mi'kmag Nation born @ 1700 buried in Port Royal Cemetery 9 February 1730.

K. Françoise born @ 1697 married (1) an unidentified @1717; m2 @ 1725 Réné Grand-Claude (Grand-Claude & Marie Medosset both of the Mi'kmag Nation)) and m3 @ 1733 Pierre Cellier called Charet. It is Stephen White's belief that this Pierre is the son of a Cellier who settled in the La Hêve area and married Mi'kmag making this couple the ancestor of the Mi'kmag branch of this family. His brother, Pierre Cellier, also married in the La Hêve region, to Marie-Josephe Le Jeune

L. Francois born @ 1700 married @ 1726 Marie of the Mi'kmag Nation. He was the Francois d'Azy Mius who signed, as Chief of the La Hêve Indians, on 9Th November1761 a Treaty of Peace between them and the British. This transaction took place in Halifax, Nova Scotia, and his counterpart was Jonathan Belcher. Francois makes another trip to Halifax 22 August1763 to request, from the Lieutenant-Governor, the appointment of another priest to minister to his Tribe since Father Maillard had been dead for a year.

M.   Philippe born @ 1703 must not have been a healthy child for there is no mention of him after the La Hêve census of 1708.

N.   Anne-Marie called Nanette born @1705 married @ 1720 Paul Guidry, brother to the ill-fated Jean-Baptiste who had married Nanette's sister, Madeleine. They had a daughter, Judique, who married 2 November1737 in Grand Pré, Jean Cousin captain of a merchant ship out of Louisbourg.

*Some of our detractors have a tendency to say that the Métis of Acadia either *Went Indian or Went White.* In the brouhaha that was stirring up in this small part of the world during the period of English *Control* on mainland Nova Scotia between the Treaty of Utrecht 1714 and the Peace Treaty of Paris of 1763, many of these people didn't know if they were coming or going anywhere at any given time. They were being pressured by the British to swear to an oath of allegiance that could see them in pitched battles with the people they shared common blood, common values, and common religion with. In the beginning the English did not want the Acadians to depart no-matter if they took the unconditional oath or not. Many Métis/Acadians and the other Acadians had taken oaths of behavior before (1695) and had *toed the line.* Though the New Englanders wanted them gone to expand their settlements and fishing options, the troops and officers depended upon Acadian produce for supplies and Acadian influence to keep the Mi'kmag in check. Our people knew that and thought that as long as they were not outnumbered by Protestant settlements in their land, nothing would change.

The British were not the only ones blowing wind their way. They were being pressured by the French to leave their homes, uproot their families, and become part of the military campaign to drive the British from what was still French Acadia. The forlorn hope that France would soon drive their enemy out of occupied Acadia if only they would help beefing up the numbers around Fort Beauséjour and Fortress Louisbourg kept being pitched at them. Some of their parish priests were trying to convince them to either overtly or covertly support the French cause. Overtly by becoming involved in the French militia or as guerilla warfare groups in league with the Mi'kmag (more about guerilla warfare later), or covertly by providing the French garrisons with beef and produce through smuggling.

Of course our brethren the Mi'kmag and their allies were not happy. They had been amazed at how easily the French kept giving up their rights in Acadia over and over again while always telling them, the Mi'kmag, that the French King would protect them from *les Anglais.* These allies were never made party to the French aspirations to maintain a huge fur trading empire in the middle of North America where the real fortunes were to be made. Louisbourg was put there to protect the fishery and the entrance to the Saint Lawrence River drainage system, their key to empire.

This lack of trust within the Mi'kmag for all Europeans was not being assuaged by the British, especially Lieutenant-Governor John Doucett (NO relationship to our Doucets). They began by taking Mi'kmag hostages hoping that this would make the non interned Natives behave. When this did not have the desired result, Doucett passed a motion through Council at Annapolis Royal on 8th July1724 that stated the following:

"It is our opinion, that since all the *kind usages* this barbarous people have received seems rather to render them more inhuman and treacherous, it will be for His Majesty's service, the security of this garrison, and the English subjects inhabiting about it, to make reprisals *by the death of one of the savage prisoners in custody,* to deter them from any further outrage, when they will lay under fear of loosing nine more still left in our possession."[55] A young man was dragged out of his cell and was hanged but the British, especially Doucett, had not read the Mi'kmag well. Revenge is inbred into their nature and this did not settle them down.

Daniel Paul, Mi'kmag author, says it right when he stated that the English despised the Acadians almost as much as his people. On 1st August1722 Richard Philipp, Governor of Acadia issued a proclamation that made it illegal for any Acadian to entertain any Mi'kmag no matter what the situation. This is what happened to one of the most respected old Acadians prior to 22 May1725: "The Honourable Lt. Governor, John Doucett, acquainted the board that Prudane Robichau, senior inhabitant in the Cape, had entertained an Indian in his house contrary to His Excellency's proclamation, dated 1 August1722. That he had therefore put him in irons in prison amongst the Indians for such heinous misdemeanor. This was to terrify the other inhabitants from clandestine practices of betraying the English subjects into Indian hands. A petition by Robichau for release was then presented to Council for approval. The said petition was read. It is the opinion of the Board, upon account of his age, and having been so long in irons, that upon the offers and promises he made in his petition of putting up as security goods and other chattels for his future good behavior, he be set free."[56] You do not get compliance through physical and mental intimidation today and I doubt that this torment of an old man had the desired effect then either. It may have further aggravated the paranoia that in the end forced Charles Lawrence to take such a radical step as he did in 1755.

I am far from done with the Mius family yet. We are about to take a look at the family of the eldest son of Philippe (2) and his first Mi'kmag wife - Joseph Mius d'Azy.

Most of his siblings married Mi'kmag partners yet because this *Bois Brule* married an Acadian woman, Marie Amireau, he is considered to be the ancestor of the Acadian branch of the Mius family. **Duh!** As parents of thirteen children who all not only reached the age of majority (adulthood), they must have been super proud of their grand children because all of these children married. This extended family forms the base for most of the people who live today on the Eastern seaboard of North America and carry Mius blood in their veins. Joseph and Marie married in the summer of 1699 and their first child was delivered the following summer.

A. Joseph (2) born in Cape Sable 27 June1700 married 9 September1726 Marie-Josephe Prejean (Jean & Andrée Savoie). This couple was deported to Salem, Massachusetts where they were joined by a seemingly lost soul by the name of Pierre Hinard (Esnard) who was seeking his own kind for solace and companionship. Born in Normandy, in the Saint Pair area, Pierre had taken an Acadian wife Marie-Josephte Bodard. Having born him three children in Pennsylvania, she passed away. In no condition to raise three infant children, Pierre deposited them with their maternal Grandmother, Marie Babin in Maryland and shipped out on a transport vessel, trying to pick up some sustenance.

Shipwrecked off Cape Cod, he heard about the Acadians in Salem and proceeded there. Hooked up with this Mius family, Pierre married @ 1765 Anne Rosalie Mius born @ 1740. They began a second family, having three children Rosalie, Marie, and Pierre. This extended family left Salem in 1767 wishing to resettle one of the capes on the west side of the Tusket River. Today this place is known as Wedgeport. Though their son Pierre never married, both of the girls did. The youngest Marie married 8 July1795 Jean-Marie Cotreau (Charles Cotreau & Jeanne Boeuf), another native of St. Pair, France, who had gotten embroiled in the early stages of the French Revolution. Taken to Halifax by the English, he *borrowed* a canoe and fled south, meeting Benoni d'Entremont, in Pubnico, who informed him that a person from his home town lived at Tusket Wedge.[57] The rest is history as they say. All Cottreau or families derived from this couple are Métis/Acadian.

B. Charles Amand (1) born in Cape Sable 17 December1702 married 31 January1731 Marie-Marthe Hébert (Antoine & Jeanne Corporon). This family also ended up in Plymouth, Massachusetts from Cape Sable in April1756. Returning to Nova Scotia in the 1760's or 1770's this couple most likely set up house in the Bellneck area just outside of Quinan. Their fourth child **Bartholemy** married Marie Madeleine Doiron in 1777. They are the dominant ancestors of all Mius, Muise, Meusse, or other derivation of this name, on the Gulf of Saint Lawrence, Chaleur Bay, Cape Breton, the Magdalene Islands, and Newfoundland. Their daughter **Magdeleine Modeste** born 1742 Baccaro, Cape Sable, died 10 February1826 Hubbard's Point, N.S., had first married Dominique Doucet (Claude & Anne Surette). Brought to Massachusetts with her parents, the widowed Magdeleine married 16 January1772 at Salem a tall thin red haired Irishman by the name of John O'Bird. He probably predeceased his wife by a couple of years in the village that still carries his name in its most common form, Hubbard's Point. Integrated into the Métis/Acadian culture, John and his wife Magdeleine are the common ancestors of all the Hubbards of Post Deportation Acadia.

C.    Francois born in Cape Sable 19 March1703 married at Port Royal,14 February1735 Jeanne Duon born 29 March1718 (Jean-Baptiste & Agnes Hébert . Jean-Baptiste was the first Duon in Acadia). Exiled to Massachusetts after being apprehended at Cape Sable in April1756, Francois was one of the first Acadians who applied to be repatriated 2 June1766. Many members of his family achieved his goal but it seems that Francois died in Salem, 1774, before the reestablishment of his line in Nova Scotia. Many people of the Yarmouth County area are descended from Francois and Jeanne. Worthy of note is their son Benjamin born 15 February1766 in Salem. He carried out his father's dream by returning to the Cape Sable region, marrying at Rocco Point, St. Anne du Ruisseau 13 June1786 Anne Doucet (Dominique & Madeleine Mius) born 15 January1759. Madeleine Mius was the daughter of Charles Amand Mius I, another case of the same blood strain continuously intermixing. Benjamin would have *La Pointe des Ben* in Sluice Point, Yarmouth County, named after him. His house is still occupied today. Another of Francois and Anne (Doucet) Mius' children worth noting is their daughter, Anne born at Port Royal 4 November1736. She married in exile in Massachusetts Alexandre Julien Frontain. All Métis/Acadians of Cape Sable with the name Frontain, Frotten, Fraughten and any other variation of this name are descended from this couple, including Leandre Frontain depicted on the front cover of this book. Their baby sister, Marie-Suzanne, born in exile @ 1758 died after 1830, married Michel Doucet born at Port Royal 17 October1754 died at Quinan 19 April1830. They probably married not long after repatriation settling first in Sluice Point where their two oldest got married then moving to the Quinan neighborhood where the rest of their children eventually settled in. Basil, son of Benjamin, nicknamed *Tachine*, had a daughter, Helene, born 1 June1847, died 6 August1911, married Alexis Vacon, native of Marseille, France. Alexis born 1812 left France as a sailor in 1840 to see the world. He set his anchor for good in Machouciak (Quinan), an inland community, where he was to sire thirteen children who have spread the name Vacon throughout Yarmouth County and beyond. I worked with his grandson Alvini, called *Minoche*, as a laborer in the Irish Moss industry in the late 1960's but this man was known for his hunting and tracking skills, at which he was excellent as were/are so many Métis/Acadians from Quinan. They could leave home with their guns, some salt and a ten pound bag of potatoes, be gone for several days and return home well fed and loaded down with game for their families.

D.    Angelique, born in Cape Sable 2 November1704 married at Port Royal, 4 January1731 Francois Grosvalet (Bertrand & Françoise Binard) Angelique died at Port Royal 19/20 March 1738 and her husband remarried 6 February1743 Madeleine Doucet (Claude & Marie Commeaux)

E.    Marie-Josephe, born in Cape Sable @ 1706 died in Quebec 14/15 December1757. Marie-Josephe married at Port Royal, 23 October1730 Jean-Baptiste Raymond (Francois & Anne Commeaux). Jean-Baptiste followed his wife to the grave less than two weeks later in Quebec. Their eldest son, Francois, and his wife Isabelle Richard ((Pierre & Isabelle Levron) married at Port Royal 18 January1753 found themselves bound for Connecticut in 1755.

F.    Claire, born @ 1709 died 9 March1760 at Cherbourg, France. Claire married 21 January1731 Charles-Paul Hébert (Antoine & Jeanne Corporon). You will notice that many of the people who made it *safely* to a destination, whether it be in Europe or somewhere in the thirteen British colonies to the south, there still was a large fatality rate amongst the *survivors*.

G.    Marie-Madeleine, born at Port Royal 28 November1710 married @ 1733 Jean-Baptiste Henry (Jean & Marie Hébert) born @ 1708. They had taken up residence at Point Prime, Ile St-Jean, in 1750 but were apprehended and placed on the transport vessel *Duke William* in 1758. This vessel and all of its occupants were lost at sea, including their seven children.

H.    Jean-Baptiste, born in 1713 married at Port Royal 3 October1736 Marie Josephte Surette (Pierre I & Jeanne Pellerin). Marie Josephte did not survive the lean years in the U.S.A. passing away in 1760. Jean-Baptiste managed to get back to Cape Sable with most of his children. His death is recorded in the St. Anne du Ruisseau Church register as having taken place at the newly founded community of Hubbard's Point on 29 June 1806. They had managed to give birth to ten children. Of special note for this publication is their third child, Laurent born @ 1739 in Baccaro, Cape Sable. He followed his family fortunes and returned to the Cape Sable region to settle in Tusket Forks, now called Quinan (Named after a popular parish priest), where his brother Jean-Baptiste (2, considered the founder, had taken up residence. Laurent married @ 1787 Marie Alexis (Michaud), a woman from the Mi'kmaq Nation. Their blood flows very strongly in the Quinan vicinity and beyond today. A sister of Laurent, Ludivine, born @ 1751 died 17 March1836 Ste Anne du Ruisseau, married @ 1754 Joseph Doucet (Claude & Marie Commeaux) also left strong Métis/Acadian ties.

I.  Marguerite born at Baccaro @ 1716 died at Quebec 5/6 October1755. In her short life Marguerite married twice: (1) @ 1734 Michel Hébert (Jean & Jeanne Doiron); (2) 29 January1753 Jean Delage called Langlois

J.  Cécile born at Port Royal 19 December1717 died Port La Joie 26 January1751. She married @ 1742 Augustin Doucet (Jean & Françoise Bourget).

K.  Genevieve born @ 1720 married @ 1746 Francois Guerin (Jerome & Isabelle Aucoin). This is another unfortunate family who perished at sea during transportation in 1758.

L.  Rosalie born at Port Royal 8 February1725 married @ 1746 Eloi Le Jeune (Pierre & Jeanne Benoit). Met the same fate as her sister Genevieve in 1758.

M.  Charles-Benjamin born at Cape Sable in April1728. The name Benjamin has the Biblical connotation in Acadia often meaning the *youngest child of my old age*. It holds very true for this family because Charles-Benjamin's father, Joseph Mius d'Azy, passed away when he was only one year old. This youngest child, this blessed child, would not be blessed with good luck either. He married @ 1749 Marie-Josephe Guedry (Augustin & Jeanne Hébert), a woman who had already been widowed once (first husband Amand Breau). These Mius's lost their lives together making that same perilous crossing that took so many of their other family members in 1758.

This Métis/Acadian family is reminiscent of so many of their people who were hard hit by Governor Charles Lawrence's heinous scheme that bore so many bitter fruit with the forced evacuation he imposed upon them beginning in 1755. *Le Grand Dérangement*, the Acadian French term for the Deportation of the Acadians is not a severe enough term to do this injustice justice. We had learned well the lessons of Jesus Christ about turning the other cheek. We came back! Throughout all the tensions and heartbreak of this massive trauma to a people just trying to live unmolested, it amazes me that our people persevered and have been able to make the positive contributions made to this part of the Earth. However, those who wish revenge or who cannot forgive and forget must let the final word be had by a mightier force in the Universe. We who have survived must move onwards.

# Chapter 6.
# Rounding Out the Group –
# Other Ancestors of the Métis/Acadians
# in the First Hundred Years.

## A. The Le Jeunes

This family, the Le Jeunes or Youngs was one of the earliest families to hire out to the fur traders, Poutrincourt or Biencourt, prior to 1620. As an *engagé*, Pierre Le Jeune came to Acadia to learn the ins and outs of the business. Included in his tasks were the boring jobs of clerking and preparing the furs for market. The more adventurous life of not only bartering with the Mi'kmag but accompanying them on the hunt and the trap lines must have lured Pierre as it did most of the young bloods in Acadia at this time. To be there first, like being in a gold rush at the beginning, encouraged these *coureurs de bois* to adapt to the language, culture, and ways of the indigenous people to achieve optimum success. Nothing like this was available in France at this time. The way that some of the Le Jeunes took to the more transient life of their Mi'kmag friends and relatives may underlie why so many of them were not found in the censuses taken, for the most part, of sedentary population bases. The close relationship experienced between these French *engagés* and the Mi'kmag of La Hêve area fostered an *esprit de famille* that made of La Hêve one of the first Métis/Acadian communities. Several other families were to join them. Pierre Le Jeune born @ 1595 married a Mi'kmag maid probably in La Hêve @ 1622. They had three children;

1) **Edmée** (Aimee) Le Jeune born @ 1624 in La Hêve married @ 1644 Francois Gauterot (Gottereau, Gautreau, Gauthreau, Gotro) in La Hêve, but they moved to Port Royal. This was Francois' second marriage for; he too, had first married a Mi'kmag maid. (One child by his first wife was: i) Marie born @ 1636 married i) @ 1656 Mr. Potet, ii) @1664 Michel Dupuis).

   **Edmée and Francois'** children were:

   a) Marie born @ 1645 died 29/30 November1732 Port Royal married @ 1661 at Port Royal Claude Theriot (Jean & Pérrine Rau. This couple is the ancestor of all the Terroit, Theriaults of Acadia). Claude died 17 September1725 at Port Royal. Claude and Edmée are the furthest back that we can trace the Métis/Acadian blood of the Theriot surname or people like me who have family ties with them.

   b) Jean born @ 1648 died young.

   c) Renée born @ 1652 died 8/9 July1737 married @ 1671 Jean Labat called *Le Marquis*. Died 19 November1714. This couple both lived to a ripe old age but they died childless, not by choice as many do today, but probably due to some medical impairment on behalf of one or the other. Back in this age your children not your bank account dictated your old age.

   d) Marguerite born @ 1654 died 2/3 August1727 married @ 1670 Jacques (Jacob) Girouard (Francois & Jeanne Aucoin) born @ 1648 died 27/28 October1703. This couple is the original Métis/Acadian link of the Girouards. They had fourteen children. Some of the families they connect to include: Granger; Doucet; Richard dit Beaupre; Gaudet; Blanchard; Guilbaut; Mouton; Forest; Dugas; Trahan; Doiron; LeBlanc; Boudrot; Pitre; Benoit; Poirier; Bourgeois; Lambert; Theriot; Thibodeau...

e) Francois born @ 1657 died before 1683 at Port Royal married @ 1677 Marie (Sebastienne) Brun (Vincent & Renée Breau)

f) Claude born @ 1659 died 24/25 March1733 married @ 1684 Marie Theriot (Bonaventure @ Jeanne Boudrot) died before 18 August1734.

g) Charles born @ 1661 died between 18 April1723 & 10 October 1725 married @ 1684 Françoise Rimbault (Réné & Anne-Marie—) died 27/28 May1712 at Grand Pré.

h) Jeanne born @ 1665 died 18/19 October1749 at Port Royal married @ 1682 Pierre Lanoue born @ 1648 died between, 1707-1714. All Lanoues stemming from this couple are Métis/Acadian.

i) Germain born @ 1668 must have died young.

2) **Pierre (2) Briard** born @ 1630 married @ 1650 a daughter of Germain (1) Doucet @ wife not identified. The **Briard** surname may well indicate the close connection between the La Jeune and Doucet family, the latter coming from **Brie**, France. This couple had at least two sons Pierre (3) and Martin, and a daughter, Jeanne, who spent a good part of their lives in the La Hêve area living in communal harmony with their Métis/Acadian friends and family. At times (1689) we find the eldest son Pierre (3) guilty of *tickling the King's beard* by getting involved in the fur trade to accommodate his brother-in-law Sieur Desgouttins, Sieur de Soulegre and his own pocket book without first seeking permission of the Governor Menneval. This system worked much like the mafia money schemes in which you had to *grease the palms* of those higher ups as a price for doing business. Menneval had forgotten to note that he had cheated the Crown out of 16 livres by passing in a voucher of 40 livres for a boat rental from Pierre Le Jeune and another settler. When Pierre found out about this discrepancy he had gone to see Mathieu de Goutin, who had replaced Michel Boudrot as the King's prosecutor general in Acadia, for the balance. This showed Menneval with *his hand caught in the cookie jar* so he wanted to make Pierre Le Jeune pay for this blight on his honor, demanding that Pierre come and explain himself and implicate his associates. Either with their help or not, Pierre and his family made themselves scarce. Pierre (3) Le Jeune called Briard born @ 1656 married before the 1678 census at Port Royal Marie Thibodeau (Pierre le meunier de la Pré Ronde & Jeanne Theriot) born @ 1663.Marie must have had to make the best of the good times and bad times as Pierre (3) would shuffle them back and forth. The family lived in La Hêve until Pierre's arrest in 1689. After 1714 they left Port Royal for Pentagouet. When you look at their history as a married couple, Marie must have had to get used to between Port Royal and La Hêve depending upon what her husband was involved in, or who he was involved with. **A) Pierre (3)** and **Marie's** children include:

a) Marie-Marguerite born @ 1687 died before 1752 married at La Hêve @ 1708 Joseph Boutin born @ 1676. They are the ancestors of the Métis/Acadian Boutins.

b) Pierre born @ 1689 married 12 September1712 at Grand Pré Jeanne Benoit (Martin & Marie Chaussegros) born @ 1692.

c) Jeanne born @ 1691 died before 1747 married 3 October1712 at Grand Pré Jean Roy (Jean & Marie Aubois/Dubois).

d) Germain born @ 1693 married i) @1717 Marie-Anne Trahan (Alexandre & Marie Pellerin); married ii) @ 1735 Marie Guedry (Jean Baptiste & Madeleine Mius d'Azy).

e) Marguerite born @ 1695 died before the census of 1752 married i) 28 November1714 at Grand Pré Alexandre Trahan ( Alexandre & Marie Pellerin) died before 18 July1746; married @ 1747 ii) Pierre Gautrot (Charles & Françoise Rimbault) widower of Marie-Josephe Bugeaud.

f) Jean born @ 1697 at Port Royal died 28 May1759 at Chateauneuf married @ 1725 Françoise Guedry (Claude & Marguerite Petitpas). Françoise was born 14 January1703 at Port Royal died 9/10 March1780 at Chantenay.

g) Anne born @ 1699. Must have died young.

h) Catherine born @ 1701 at Port Royal married i) at Grand Pré 10 October1718 Antoine Labauve (Louis-Noel & Marie Rimbault) born @ 1690 died 26/27 April1733 at Louisbourg. Catherine married ii) Claude–Antoine Duplessis (Claude-Antoine & Marie Derivi)

i) Joseph born 20 July1704 married @ 1727 Cécile Pitre (Jean & Françoise Babin). This couple and whatever members of their extended family that happened to be with them were lost at sea in the transport vessel *Violet* 13 December1758 on their way to France during the Deportation.

B) **Martin called Briard (Labriere)** born @ 1661 married @ 1684 i) **Jeanne (Marie) Kagigconiac of the First Nations**. Martin married ii) 1699 **Marie Gaudet** (Jean & Jeanne Henry) married iii) 16 October1729 at Grand Pre **Marie Arnault (Renaud)**. This third wife would be the companion of his old age and not produce any offspring

**Married i) Jeanne (Marie) Kagigconiac:**

a) Claude called Briard born 1686 at La Hêve died before 19 November1725 married 14 September1705 at Port Royal Anne-Marie Gaudet (Jean & Jeanne Henry), his stepmother's younger sister. They had only two daughters Marie-Josephe and Marguerite who married into the (Martin) Benoit and (Charles) Roy families respectively.

b) Daughter born before the census of 1686 but did not survive

c) Anne called Briard born @ 1687 married @ 1702 Réné (called Renochon) Labauve (Louis-Noel & Marie Rimbault). Their eldest daughter, Marie (-Josephe) born 1706 married @ 1728 Francois LeBlanc (André & Marie Dugas) their youngest daughter, Cécile married @ 1735 Jean-Baptiste Orillon called *Champagne,* the elder (Charles & Marie-Anne Bastarache). By 1760 this family was in Quebec.

d) Germain born @ 1689. In the 1708 census he is residing at La Hêve and is of marriageable age (19). He may have married First Nation.

e) Bernard born @ 1693 is listed at age 15 in the 1708 La Hêve census. He is another young man who was lost in the cracks of the census taking methods of the time.

Married ii) Marie Gaudet

f) Theodore born @ 1700 died before 1752 married @ 1721 Daughter of Jean Landry and Cécile Melanson of Pisiguit (Windsor, N. S.). Cécile is the daughter of Charles Melanson and Marie Dugas. This Daughter may carry her mother or her grandmother's name.

g) Paul called Briard born a twin 9 October1702 died before the census of 1761 married @ 1724 Marie Benoit (Pierre the younger & Elisabeth Le Juge). Paul's Godparents were Jean-Baptiste Guedry and Marguerite Kagigconiac. The Le Jeune family was living in Port-Maltais, Cape Sable at the time.

h) Martin the other twin born 9 October1702. His Godparents were Germain Le Jeune and Catherine Kagigconiac so, like his half-brother, young Martin's life, if indeed he had one, could have been a life of food gathering with the Mi'kmag of the La Hêve area.

i) Claire born @ 1706 died before 23 November1768 married @ 1722 Francois Viger (Francois & Marie Mius).

j) Marguerite born 9 July1710. She may have died young. Marguerite and her two younger brothers can be found in the Grand Pré church records.

k) Eustache called Briard born August1715 died before 1760 married Marie-Anne Barrieau (Jacques & Anne-Marie Turpin).

l) Pierre born @ 1719 was only registered at Grand Pré 16 September1736 when he was seventeen years of age. This in itself shows the turbulence this family experienced willingly, or unwillingly, during the first stage of British dominance.

3) **Catherine Le Jeune called Briard** born @ 1633 on Acadian soil. Catherine married @ 1651 **Francois Savoie** born @ 1621 Loudunois, Poitou, France. Francois came to Acadia as an *engagé* of Charles de Menou d'Aulnay @ 1643, the first of this surname to cross the Atlantic as a laborer/settler. Of humble origins this family sowed the seed that was to make Savoie (Savoy, Savoye, Savoix, Savois, Scavoie, Scavois etc.) well known in Canada and other parts of North America. Francois and Catherine have nine children, three boys and six girls. Two of these daughters, Françoise and Jeanne were to become the matriarchs of two new Métis/Acadian families that play important roles in the story of the Cape Sable region. Those families are the Corporon and the Suret (Surette). Through these two families the Le Jeune and First Nation blood flows strongly to this day. Large families intermarrying with a fixed amount of other large families in a relatively small area has guaranteed this trend. **Catherine Le Jeune & Francois Savoie** had the following children:

A) Françoise born @ 1652 died 27 December1711 at Port Royal married @ 1670 Jean Corporon died 12 February1712 at Port Royal. They established themselves in Port Royal next to Jehan Terriau & Pérrine Bourg and the Savoie homestead. Their sons Jean (-Baptiste) and Martin would establish themselves in Pisiguit. Jean born @ 1677, a *Jack-of-all-Trades* was as comfortable on sea as he was on land. He married @1702 Marie Pinet born 8 October1685 in the Minas Basin died Isle Royale/Cape Breton 15/16 December1732 (Philippe & Catherine Hébert). Of special note to the people of Cape Sable is their son **Eustache** born @ 1725 married @ 1749 Angelique Viger called Brigeau (Francois & Claire Le Jeune). It is uncertain whether Eustache was deported or not yet the historian, Rev. J.R Campbell, ascertains that it was he who piloted an English crew in the Tusket River/Argyle region seeking out Acadian/ Mi'kmag residents." After exploring the shores of the Tusket River, they went to Argyle, at the time called *Papgogteg*, where the crew landed on a marsh where there were some sheep. The Micmacs ambushed the crew and killed eight of them. Eustache Corporon fled into the forest with the Micmacs."[58] By1763 he is a captive in Halifax, his family included with the many other families that had finally given up any hope of a French comeback in Acadia or any other part of Canada.

The fall of the Fortress Quebec had scuttled the hopes of many; Montreal's loss was the last nail on the coffin. There was nowhere left to hide that *Les Anglais* could not eventually find and destroy. One of his daughters Marie Rose, born @ 1752, married Pierre Cadet (Jr.) Robichaud, born in 1737, son of Pierre Robichaud Sr. (1707) and Suzanne Brasseau. The Senior Robichaud couple had started out at Port Royal, moved to Cobiquid (Truro, N.S.), following the advice of the French, removed themselves and all that they owned to *La Rivière des Blonds* (Tyron River, P.E.I.) and by 1769 found themselves in the Halifax /Dartmouth area with the Corporons. The Junior Robichauds finally moved themselves to the newly founded Wedgeport community where they had lands given to them by other members of their family. Eustache followed their lead and settled an old Mi'kmag site *Chebec (Thebec)* where the cape retains its Corporon name to this day.

B) Germain born @ 1654 died after pledging allegiance December1729 married @1678 Marie Breau called Vincelotte (Vincent & Marie Bourg) born @1662 died at Port Royal 23/24 October1749.

C) Marie born @ 1657 died Louisbourg 10/11 March 1741 married @ 1676 Jacques Triel called Laperriere born @1646 died before the 1700 census.

D) **Jeanne** born @ 1658 died 3/4 November1735 married @1675 **Étienne Pellerin** born 1646 France died 17 November1722. Étienne is the founder of the Métis/Acadian branch of the Pellerins in Acadia. Both of these people were buried in Port Royal. **Étienne** and **Jeanne's** children include the following:

a) Madeleine born @ 1676 married i) @ 1693 Charles Calve called Laforge died childless 29/30 September1705; married ii) 17 January1707 at Port Royal to Pierre Gaudet called Will Denis born @ 1676 (Pierre Gaudet, the younger & Marie Blanchard ). This couple failed to have any children.

b) Marie born @ 1678 married @ 1695 Jacques Doucet called Maillard (Germain & Marie Landry) This couple had eleven children six who would go on to raise families.

c) Pierre born @ 1682. He is lost sight of after the census of 1701 and may have joined the Mi'kmag Nation.

d) Anne born @ 1684 married i) @ 1701 Abraham Brun (Sebastien & Huguette Bourg); married ii) 12 January1722 at Port Royal Laurent Doucet (Laurent & Jeanne Babin).

e) Jean-Baptiste born @ 1685 married 11 February1710 Marie Martin (Pierre & Anne Ouestnorouest a First Nation maid). Marie born @ 1678 died 11/12 November1746.

f) **Jeanne born** @ 1688 died in Quebec 27/28 January1758.married 4 February1709

**Pierre I** Surette (Noel & Françoise Colarde) born @ 1679 died at Port Royal 30/31 October1749. Pierre, a sailor by trade, a farmer by inclination, took very little time to put a bee in Jeanne's bonnet for he had only arrived in Acadia from Mauset, Diocese of La Rochelle, in 1708. He had not only gotten married in 1709, his first son Pierre II was born, the first Métis/Acadian of the Surette family arriving just in time for Christmas. The newlyweds set up housekeeping not far from the Saint Laurent parish chapel, a distance up from the Port Royal (Annapolis) River. This renaming of the river did not take place many years after the Surette's tried to build a family and carve out a home in this new world. France's inability to hold on to this part of Acadia would be a source of torment for generations of Surette's yet unborn. All Métis/Acadians with the Surette surname or any derivative thereof are descended from Pierre I and Jeanne Pellerin.

# B. The Dugast (Dugas)

Abraham Dugas or Habraham Dugast was born 1616 at Toulouse in the Languedoc region of France. Some state that his family originated in Lyon where the order of Saint Louis and a grant of land was bequeathed to this earlier member whose surname was Coignet, the grant being called *le domaine du Gas.* Abraham's family carried the surname Coignet du Gas but eventually it was tailored to just Dugas. He had set up at Toulouse as one of the King's armorers, producing equipment and guns of the era. He was still a bachelor when he uprooted himself and tied his star to Charles de Menou in 1640, looking to see what he could gain for himself, and perhaps, those who would follow this bold jump into the new world Acadia offered. He knew that his skills would not get *rusty* with so much action flaring up between the English and the French, the French and the French (d'Aulnay, La Tour, and Denys). From the time of his arrival until 1654 when the Bostonians took over, Abraham therefore kept busy supplying guns and the paraphernalia that go with them for both the military and the civilian population who required them for hunting as well as protection.

One of d'Aulnay's picked men, Abraham, was closely associated with the other picked men and in 1647 he married into the Doucet/Bourgeois family when he took the hand in marriage of Marguerite Doucet (Germain I & Marie Bourgeois) born 1625 Couperans-Brie Sinking roots in Acadia, Abraham and his wife begin a family and build a prosperous farm to house the eight children they were to have over the next twenty years. I intend to list nine of these children and focus on the other, the branch that would reproduce Métis/Acadians in the region known as Clare to some, Par-en-Haut to others. Abraham Dugas was to achieve considerable status in Port Royal, briefly being named Justice of the Peace and Lieutenant-General in charge of police matters in Acadia from 1685 to 1686 when the census was taken and at 70 years young, he was replaced by Michel Boudrot. Abraham was also one of the *anciens habitants du pays* who bore witness, on 15 October1687, to the works of his old mentor, Charles de Menou, Sieur d'Aulnay-Charnisay, while he had been Governor of Acadia. Abraham was to die around the age of 80 before the census of 1700. His wife, Marguerite, would live on until 19/20 December1707, and be interred in the upper reaches of the river at the Saint-Laurent Chapel.

**Abraham** and **Marguerite's** children are as follows:

1) **Marie** born circa 1648 died 7/8 July1737 Port Royal married circa 1663 Charles **Melanson** (Pierre & Priscilla) called La Ramee died 1700/1701 Port Royal.

2) **Claude** born circa 1649 died 16 October1732 Port Royal married (i) circa 1673 Françoise **Bourgeois** (Jacques & Jeanne Trahan) married (ii) circa 1697 Marguerite **Bourg** (Bernard & Françoise Brun). As you can see Claude married twice. Bona Arsenault (p 394) gives him and his first wife Françoise credit for their twelve children but does not mention the other ten children Claude and second wife, Marguerite, had, found in Stephen A. White's geneology. The first group holds a special person for the people of Clare. He is **Francois** born circa 1688 married 24 October1713 **Claire Bourg** (Bernard & Françoise Brun). They gave birth 26 August1714 to **Louis called Plaisent,** who married 14 February1740 at Port Royal, **Cécile Girouard** (Alexandre & Marie Le Borgne de Belisle). These are the parents of **Joseph Dugas** born 1745 married 1762 (Marriage ratified Baie Sainte-Marie 19 September1769) **Marie-Josephe Robichaud** (Prudent & Marie-Josephe Richard). This Métis/Acadian Joseph Dugas is considered to be one of the first settlers on la Baie Saint-Marie, establishing themselves at l'Anse des LeBlanc in 1769. The Acadian School, *Joseph Dugas,* located at Church Point commemorates his name.

3) **Anne** born circa 1654 died 4/5 November1740 Beaubassin married (i) circa 1668 Charles **Bourgeois** (Jacques & Jeanne Trahan) married (ii) 26 April1679 Jean-Aubin **Mignot** called **Chatillon** (Jean & Louise Cloutier).

4) **Martin** born circa 1656 died circa 1680 married circa 1677 Marguerite Petitpas (Claude I & Catherine Bugaret) born circa 1661. Widowed young with two babies, Marguerite married circa 1681 Claude **Guedry** called both Grivois and Laverdure. Though there are many other Métis/Acadian descendents from other branches of the Dugas family, we will pause here a second to peek at Martin's family that, in earlier days, had been absorbed into another branch because it had been felt that Martin, dead as a young man, had died celibate. Stephen A. White, and his research team, deserves all the kudos for this one. Par-en-Haut, you are called Joseph a Louis a Francois a Claude a Abraham much more often than Joseph Dugas. There are so many Dugas, Comeau, Deveau, LeBlanc, Doucet, Robichaud, Theriault, in La Ville Francaise, as Clare, with all of its closely connected villages, were first called that to simply give your first and family name is quite often insufficient. It is amazing how the locals hardly ever get confused because names like Joseph are very commonly used by all of these families. Martin and Marguerite only had two children:

A) **Abraham** .born circa 1678 died 3 May1720 greater Port Royal married circa 1702 **Marie-Madeleine Landry** (Claude & Marguerite Teriot) born July 1684 died circa 1717. Though Abraham died after a long illness and Marie-Madeleine succumbed in her early thirties, their six children would all grow up to start families of their own. Several of them would become ancestors of the Dugas in Louisiana.

B) **Marguerite** born circa 1680 married (i) circa 1697 in Acadia **Joseph Guyon (Dion)** born 16 January1674 Quebec died 15 September1714; married (ii) 23 May 1717 at Louisbourg **Francois Cressonnet called Beauséjour** (Leonard & Marie- Madeleine Volondat). The first marriage produced four children. At least two were to be married.

5) **Marguerite** born circa 1657 died before 1686 married circa 1675 **Pierre Arseneau** born circa 1650 died before census of 1714. Children: **Pierre** born 1676 and **Abraham,** born 1678.

6) **Abraham** born circa 1661 died after the 1734 census married 1685 **Jeanne Guilbeau** (Pierre & Catherine Terriot) born circa 1670. They resided in Cape Sable.

7) **Madeleine** born circa 1664 died 8/9 August1738 at Port Royal married 1682 **Germain Bourgeois** (Jacques & Jeanne Trahan), his second wife. Germain, according to Stephen A. White, a middle classed merchant (which is what the term *bourgeois* stands for) who died while Father Durand was held captive at Boston.

8) **Marie** born circa 1667 died 13/14 January1734 Grand Pré married 1683 **André LeBlanc** (Daniel & Françoise Gaudet) born circa 1671 died 4/5 May 1743 Grand Pré.

As one goes through the many shoots that sprouted from the Dugas family tree, the families that they ally themselves with is almost a panorama of the Acadian families of Old Acadie.

# C. The Petitpas

The patriarch of the Petitpas name in Acadia went by the name of **Claude**, a man born on French soil in 1624, who came to Acadia at a young age and never looked back. Claude was another person who loved the freedom and life of adventure to be had in this part of the world. He found here that once out in the countryside the rule book could be *thrown out the window* and, when with the Mi'kmag, a man could become as big as his shoe size allowed him. Like the Le Jeunes and the Martins, Claude became an accepted associate of this First Nation, beginning a trend that many of his sons would follow. In Acadia since 1645, Claude only married **Catherine Bugaret** in 1658 when he started to settle down, being appointed court recorder and given the title of **Sieur de La Fleur**. How many children did he sire before this marriage with Mi'kmag women? We do know that Claude brought his *legitimate* sons with him to see the ways of this friendly people and the other Métis/Acadian families that lived with them. **Rameau de Saint Père**, a Frenchman who published a major work, *Une colonie feodale en Amerique* (Montreal, 1889) makes a typically bourgeois statement about the Petitpas which goes like this: "All the pleasures, all the souvenirs of their youth, thus left in their minds, the strong image of this nomad life, careless, accident prone, that easily lead men, brings them astray from civilized traditions, and gradually leads them to savagery. Such an irresistible drive, they never come back! Also, while the daughters of Petitpas married at Port Royal, none of the sons stayed, none were tempted by the rich territories of the Mines, none directed themselves towards the immense pastures of Beaubassin: but we find them on the desert and rugged shores of La Hêve, and it is in this way that a family, which was sure to figure among the most notable of the colony, got wrecked among the hunters, the fishermen and the wood runners." At least Saint Père and I agree on one thing, that anyone who finds Petitpas in his family tree stands an excellent chance of being Métis.

Here is an accounting of the children of **Claude (1) & Catherine**:

1) **Bernard** born circa 1659 married circa 1685 an **Unknown Woman**, though she is said to be born 1668, took part in the census of Merliguesh 1686. One must assume that since no Acadian name was attributed to her, she must be Mi'kmag.

2) **Marguerite** born circa 1661 Port Royal married (i) 1677 **Martin Dugas** (Abraham & Marguerite Doucet) married (ii) 1681 **Claude Guedry dit Grivois dit Laverdure**

3) **Claude** born circa 1663 died circa 1731 married (i) before the census 1686 **Marie-Therese (Mi'kmag)** born circa 1668 died before1717 census married (ii) **Françoise Lavergne** ( Pierre & Anne Bernon) born 2 April1703 Port Royal died after 30 September1771.

4) **Jean** born circa 1664. May have died young

5) **Jacques** born circa 1666 died 1694 married circa1690 **Genevieve Serreau de Saint-Aubin** (Jean & Marguerite Boileau)

6) **Marie** born circa May 1669 Port Royal died before 1707 census married circa 1689 **Michel de Forest** (Michel & Marie Hébert) born circa 1667 died before 2 July1731 Michel's second marriage 29 October1708 at Grand Pré **Marie Celestin dit Bellemere** (André & Pérrine Basile)

7) **Isabelle (Elisabeth)** born circa 1670 married (i) 1686 **Olivier Boudrot** (Michel & Michelle Aucoin) born circa 1661 died before 1690 married (ii) circa 1690 **Alexandre Richard** (Michel & Madeleine Blanchard) born circa 1668 died 4/6 October1709

8) **Henriette** born circa 1674 married circa 1691 **Prudent Robichaud** ( Étienne & Françoise Boudrot) born circa 1669 died 1756

9) **Paul** born circa 1675, 22 years of in the census of 1693

10) **Charles** born circa 1676, 18 years old in the census of 1693

11) **Martin** born circa 1677, listed as 15 years old census 1693

12) **Pierre** born circa 1681, listed as 10 years old census of 1693

* All four of the abovementioned boys did not fall off the face of the Earth in 1693. The most probable outcome is that they lived the free life of the Métis and did not want to return to an Acadian settlement to be counted.

13) **Anne** born circa 1684 died 14 October 1717 Port Royal married 3 November 1704 Port Royal **Jacques Girouard** (Jacques & Marguerite Gautrot).

The Petitpas are certainly not the last of the early Métis/Acadian families. As good a showing can be made for the Roy, the Martin and to, a lesser degree the LeBlanc, the Gaudet, the Richard, the Boudreau, and several families not yet mentioned in the upcoming Acadian Census of 1671. Each generation of these prolific families must be carefully gone over to find and follow the Métis bloodlines. Time constraints demand that I stop here but, if truly wanting to know what is in your blood, go to a library, a bookstore or on line. If you look long enough and hard enough, your questions will be answered. This may prove, or disprove, your aboriginal links but, just as much as people like to know who they are and where they come from, the satisfaction comes with the knowing.

# D. The 1671 Acadian Census

It is impossible for me to include all of the censuses taken in Acadia because it would pull us away from the original premise this book is built on. However, this first audit, compiled by Father Laurent Molin for the new Governor of New France (Quebec), Sieur Hector d'Andigne de Grandfontaine, gives a good overall view of the *recorded* families in Acadia as of 1671. Here we go:

Jacob Bourgeois, Surgeon, 50: wife Jeanne Trahan 40; Children; two of them married: Jeanne 27, and Charles 25; then Germain 21, Marie 19, Guillaume 16, Marguerite 13, Francois 12, Anne 10, Marie 7, Jeanne 4; cattle 33, sheep 24.

Jean Gaudet, farmer, 96, wife, Nicolle Colleson 64; Child: Jehan 18, cattle 6, sheep 3.

Denis Gaudet, 46, wife Martine Gauthier 62; Children (the first two married): Anne 25, Marie 21, Pierre 20, Pierre 17, Marie 14; cattle 9, sheep 13.

Roger Kuessy, 25, wife Marie Poirier 22, Child: Marie 2; cattle 3, sheep 2.

Michel De Forest 33, wife Marie Hébert 20; Children: Michel 4, Pierre 2, Réné 1; cattle 12, sheep 2.

Marie Gaudet, Widow of Étienne Hébert, 38, Children (married): Marie 20, Marguerite 19; (not married): Emmanuel 17, Étienne 17, Jean 13, Françoise 10, Catherine 9, Martine 6, Michel 5, Antoine 1; cattle 4, sheep 5.

Antoine Babin 45, wife Marie Mercier 25; Children: Marie 9, Charles 7, Vincent 5, Jeanne 3, Marguerite 1 cattle 6, sheep 8.

Olivier Daigre 28, wife Marie Gaudet 20: Children: Jean 4, Jacques 2, Bernard 1: cattle 6, sheep 6.

Antoine Hébert, cooper, 50, wife Genevieve Lefrance 58; Children: Jehan 22, Jehan 18, Catherine 15; cattle 18, sheep 7, 6 arpents (acres) in 2 places.

Jehan Blanchard, 60, wife Radegonde Lambert 42 ; Children (married) Martin 24, Madeline 28, Anne 26; (unmarried): Guillaume 21, Bernard 18, Marie 15; cattle 12, sheep 9.

Widow Francois Aucoin (Guerin), 26; Children: Anne 12, Marie 9, Frivoline (Jerome) 7, Huguetta 5, Francois 2: cattle 6, sheep 3, 6 arpents.

Michel Dupont (Dupuis), 37, wife Marie Gauterot 34; Children: Marie 14, Martin 6, Jeanne 4, Pierre 3; cattle 5, sheep 1, 6 arpents.

Claude Terriau, 34, wife Marie Gauterot, 24; Children: Germain 9, Marie 6, Marguerite 4, Jean 1; cattle 13, sheep 3, 6 arpents.

Germain Terriau, 25, wife Andrée Brun 25; Children: Germain2; cattle 5, sheep 2, 2 arpents.

Jean Terriau, 70, wife Pérrine Rau (Breau) 60; Children: (married) Claude 34, Jean 32, Bonaventure 30, Germain25, Jeanne 27, Catherine 21; (not married): Pierre 16; cattle 6, sheep 1.

Francois Scavois (Savoye), 50, wife Catherine LeJeune 38; Children: Françoise 18, Germain 16, Marie 14, Jeanne 13, Catherine 9, Françoise 8, Barnabé 6, André 4, Marie 2; cattle 4.

Jehhan Corporon, 25, wife Françoise Scavoie (Savoie) 18; Child: one daughter of six weeks not yet named; cattle 1, sheep 1.

Pierre Martin, 70, wife Catherine Vigneau 68; Children (married): Pierre 45, Marie 35, Marguerite 32, André 30, (not married): Mathier (Mathieu) 35; cattle 7, sheep 8.

Francois Pelerin, 35, wife Andrée Martin 30; Children: Huguette 5, Marie 2, infant girl 2 days; sheep 1.

Pierre Morin, 37, wife Marie Martin 35; Children: Pierre 9, Louis 7, Antoine 5, Marie 3, Anne ten months; cattle 3, sheep 4

Mathieu Martin, 35, not married and a weaver cattle 4, sheep 3.

Vincent Brun 60, wife Renée Brode 55; Children (married): Madeline 25, Andrée 24, Françoise 18; (not Married): Bastien 15, Marie 12; cattle 10, sheep 4.

Francois Gauterot, 58, wife Edmée Le Jeune 47; Children (married): Marie 35, Charles 34, Marie 24, Réné 19, Marguerite 16; (not married): Jean 23, Francois 19, Claude 12, Charles 10, Jeanne 7 Germain 3; cattle 16, sheep 6.

Guillaume Trahan, 60, wife Madelaine Brun 25; Children: Guillaume 4, Jehan-Charles 3, Alexandre 1; cattle 8, sheep 10.

Pierre Sire (Cyr) 27, gunsmith, wife Marie Bourgeois 18; Child: Jean 3 months; cattle 11, sheep 6.

Pierre Thibeaudeau, 40, wife Jeanne Terriau 27; Children: Pierre 1, Marie 10, Marie 9, Marie 7, Anne Marie 6, Catherine 4; cattle 12, sheep 11.

Claude Petitpas, 45, Catherine Bagard (Bugaret) 33; Children Bernard 12, Claude 8, Jean 7, Jacques 5, Marguerite 10, Marie 2, Elisabeth 1; cattle 26, sheep 11.

Bernard Bour (Bourque), 23, wife Françoise Brun 19; Child: Marie; cattle 6, sheep 9.

Bonaventure Terriau, 27, wife Jeanne Boudrot 26; Child: Marie 4; cattle 6, sheep 6.

Michel Boudrot, 71, wife Michelle Aucoin 53; Children (three married): Françoise 29, Jeanne 25, Marguerite 20; (these not married): Charles 22, Marie 18, Jehan 16, Abraham 14, Michel 12, Olivier 10, Claude 8, Francois 5; cattle 5, sheep 12.

Pierre Guilbault, 32, wife Catherine Terriau 20; Child: Marguerite 2; cattle 6, sheep 5.

Jehan Labatte, 33, wife Renée Gautherot 19 cattle 26, sheep15.

Martin Blanchard, 24, wife Françoise LeBlanc 18 cattle 5, sheep 2.

Jehan Bour, 26, wife Marguerite Martin 27; Children: Anne 3, Marguerite 1-1/2; cattle 3, sheep 5.

Antoine Bourg, 62, wife Antoinette Landry, 53; Children (4 married): Marie 26, Francois 27, Jehan 24, Bernard 22; (not Married): Martin 21, Jeanne 18, Renée 16, Huguette 14, Jeanne 12, Abraham 9, Marguerite 4; cattle 12, sheep 8.

Laurent Grange (Granger), 34, wife Marie Landry 24; Children: Marguerite 3, Pierre 9 months; cattle 5, sheep 6.

Pérrine Landry, 60, widow of Jacques Joffriau. No Children.

Pierre Doucet, bricklayer 50, wife Henriette Peltret 31; Children Anne 10, Toussaint 8, Jean 6, Pierre 4, and 1 daughter 3 months; cattle 7, sheep 6.

Francois Bour, 28, wife Marguerite Boudrot 23; Children: Michel 5, Marie 3; cattle 15, sheep.

Marie Sale, 61, widow of Jehan Claude.

Germain Doucet, 30, wife Marie Landry 24; Children Charles 6, Bernard 4, Laurent 3; cattle 11, sheep 7.

Francois Girouard, 50, wife Jeanne Aucoin 40; Children (three married): Jacob 23, Marie 20, Marie Magdeleine 17; (not Married): Germain 14, Anne 12; cattle 16, sheep 12.

Jacques Belou, cooper, 30, wife Marie Girouard 20; Child: Marie 8 months; cattle 7, sheep 1.

Jacob Girouard, 23, wife Marguerite Gautrot; Child: Alexandre; cattle 7, sheep 3.

Pierre Vincent, 40, wife Anne Gaudet; Children: Huguette 7, Thomas 6, Michel 3, Pierre 2; cattle 18, sheep 9.

Pierre Martin, 40, wife Anne Ouestnorouest 27; Children: Pierre 10, Réné 8, André 5, Jacques 2; cattle 11, sheep 9.

Vincent Brot (Breau), 40, wife Marie Bourg, 26; Children: Marie 9, Antoine 5, Marguerite 3, Pierre 1; cattle 9, sheep 7.

Daniel LeBlanc, 45, wife Françoise Gaudet 48; Children (I married): Françoise 18; (not married) Jacques 20, Étienne 15, Réné 14, André 12, Antoine 9, Pierre 7; cattle 17, sheep 26.

Michel Poirier, 20, son of the deceased Jehan Poirier; cattle 2, no sheep.

Barbe Baiolet, 63, widow of Savinien de Courpon; Children: 6 children in France and elsewhere and 2 daughters in this country. The two in this country are two married daughters Marie Peselet 26, and Marianne Lefebvre 21; cattle 7, cow 1, sheep 5.

Antoine Gougeon, 45, wife Jeanne Chebrat 45; Child: Huguette 14; cattle 20, sheep 17.

Pierre Commeaux, cooper, 75, wife Rose Bayols; Children (1 married) Étienne 21; (not married): Pierre 18, Françoise 15, Jehan 14, Pierre 13, Antoine 10, Jeanne 9, Marie 7, Jehan 6; cattle 16, sheep 22.

Jean Pitre, edge tool maker, 35, wife Marie Peselet 26; Children: Marie 5, Catherine 3, Claude 9 months; cattle 1.

Étienne Commeaux, farmer, 21, wife, Marie Anne Lefebvre 21; 1 child: Catherine, 3weeks; cattle 7, sheep 7.

Charles Bourgeois, 25, wife Anne Dugast 17; Child: Marie 2; cattle 12, sheep 6.

Barnabé Martin, 35, wife Jeanne Pelletrot 27; Children: Marie 4, Réné 8 months; cattle 3, sheep 2.

Clement Bertrant carpenter 50, wife Huguette Lambelot 48; cattle 10, sheep 6.

Antoine Belliveau, 50, wife Andrée Guion 56; Children: jean 19, Magdeleine 17; cattle 11, sheep 8.

René Landry, 52, wife Pérrine Bourg, 45; Children (4 married): Henriette Pelletrot 30, Jeanne 28, Marie 25, Marie 23; (not married): Magdeleine 15, Pierre 13, Claude 8; cattle 10, sheep 6.

Thomas Cormier, carpenter, 35, wife Madeleine Girouard 17; Child: 1 daughter 2; cattle 7, sheep 7.

René Rimbault, 55, wife Anne Marie 40; Children: Philippe 16, Francois 15, Jeanne 11, Marie 10, Françoise 5; cattle 12 sheep 9.

Abraham Dugast, gunsmith, 55, wife Marie Judith Doucet 46; Children: Claude 19, Martin, 15, Abraham 10, Marie 23, Anne 17, Marguerite 14, Magdeleine 7, Marie 5; cattle 1, sheep 3.

Michel Richard, 41, wife Madeleine Blanchard 28; Children: René 14, Pierre 10, Martin 6, Alexandre 3, Catherine 8, Anne and Madeleine 5 weeks; cattle 15, sheep 14.

Charles Melanson, 28, wife Marie Dugast 23; Children: Marie 7, Marguerite 5, Anne 3, Cécile 6 months; cattle 40, sheep 6.

Pierre Melancon, tailor – He refused to answer. (He had a wife and 7 children). Pierre would not give his age or the number of animals. His wife asked the Sieur taking the census if he was crazy to run through the streets for such information.

Étienne Robichaut, farmer, did not want to see him either. He came out and told his wife that he did not want to give account of his cattle or land.

Pierre Lanoue, cooper, sent word that he was feeling fine and he did not want to give his age.

THE HABITATION OF POBONCOM (Near the Island of Touquet)

Phillippe Mius, squire, Sieur de Landremont, 62, wife Madeleine Élie; Children: Abraham 13, Phillippe 11, another of 17, and 2 daughters; cattle 26; sheep 25.

CAPE NEGRE

Armond Lalloue, Sieur de Derivedu, 58, wife Elisabeth Nicolas; Children: Jacques 24, Amond 14, Arnault 12, and 2 daughters.

RIVIÈRE AUX ROCHELOIS

Guillaume Poulet, wife and 1 child.

TOTAL MEN, WOMEN and CHILDREN: 392

TOTAL CATTLE: 482   TOTAL

SHEEP: (I lost count of the sheep many times doing this project) 524

So went the census of 1671. It shows the intermarriage patterns of Old Acadie held true when we were allowed to return. Families tended to group their homes together thus forming the nuclei of new villages, intermarriage reinforced these family ties and extended the families throughout certain regions like Clare, the Pubnicos, and the other Acadian villages of Yarmouth County. It would not take an *outsider* long to notice the difference in the local *patois* (linguistic variance) between Meteghen, Wedgeport or West Pubnico.

What should not go unnoticed here are the names of families that should have been included in the 1671 census but weren't. That some type of enumeration for Pubnico, Cape Negre, and Rivière aux Rochelois did take place does not explain why such long established communities like La Hêve were not. Was this a racial bias in that La Hêve, due to the strong family links that existed between the Mi'kmag and Acadians, were watering down their personal value? Most, but not all, of the information does not a good census make.

One cannot help but notice that not all people asked became willing participants of this census. Melanson, Robichaud and Lanoue may have smelled a rat in an era when this type of information had no perceived benefit for the common good. Giving exact information on the number of people and their goods out to a Crown that was constantly trading this region back and forth for bigger payouts into the royal coffers might leave the residents ill at ease. These early inhabitants may have been thinking of making something permanent for future generations. A fair amount of them were literate but I doubt that they could envision a time when people like us would be scrounging for any bits of information left by their presence in this new world environment, so different from the old country, where Frenchmen could choose to ignore the directives of their King and know that they could get away with it.

# Chapter 7.
# The Good Years, the Bad Years for all our Peoples of Acadia up to 1763

## A. From the Treaty of Utrecht to the early 1750's

One of the main reasons for writing the book using this mixture of history and geneology is to demonstrate where the various branches of the Métis/Acadian families were **born**, how they developed and how the events of the day dictated how and where these families ended up. Depending upon the political situation that existed from 1713, with both France and England trying to cloud the exact location of the Acadia ceded to the English in the Treaty of Utrecht, there were many options open to these families with most being **pipe dreams** that King Louis XV's administrators kept the Acadians hopes up with. They were not being fair to these people in the least for France's upper crust was lusting for the riches up the Saint Lawrence River system and west to the Ohio and Mississippi fur empires. Nor could the residents in Acadia understand that the expected riches of India and the Orient were of more importance to the French elite than the furs, fish, and lands of the Americas. Had not these new lands originally been seen as an impediment to the spices and luxuries of Marco Polo's Kublai Khan and not a stroke of good luck in its own right? Good King Louis XV had married Marie Leczinska, daughter of Stanislas, the deposed King of Poland who was to give him ten children.[59]

As he grew older, King Louis was lusting of a much more carnal nature. His appetite for feminine conquests permeated his reign so much so that he was to have over one hundred mistresses who came from all levels of society. He even demanded that parents preserve the virginity of under aged children until **He** was ready. His Valet de Chambre, M. LeBelle, would keep tabs for him. Louis would also chase nude women with his hounds to give some variety to his *Chassee la Femme* routines. It is important to know about Louis XV, the person, because two years after the signing of the Treaty of Utrecht, this man became King of France at the tender age of five. He was to remain King until his death in 1774. Perhaps in part due to the length of time that his empire was under the rule of regents with special interests, he grew up to become a weak willed individual who allowed others to dictate policy for him. King Louis assumed the role of absolute ruler of the French worldwide without the tools of a chess master capable of playing at least two chess boards at the same time. There were constant skirmishes in Canada and India between the English and the French yet Louis never deployed enough pieces on land or on sea to make the game even ended. Under such a master, it is no wonder that the French colonial empire was doomed to self implode.

Louis XV's most prudent advisor was Cardinal Fleury who stabilized the currency of France thus facilitating trade, business and industry. However, even the Roman Catholic Religion in France had cancers that the Cardinal dared not advise the King to suppress. "The doctrine of the Bishop of Ypres, Jansenious, became quite widely accepted in France. He held that divine grace is denied or granted to all Christians in accordance with predestination. Jansenism had been adopted by men of great virtue, like the Arnauld, and had spread to certain religious houses (Port Royal). The Jansenists were opposed to the indulgence of the Jesuits..."[60] A crucifix of this cult was one with the arms not fully extended. Such a crucifix was found in the ruins of Cape Sable. Were the de La Tours believers of this doctrine?

The King, who was an advocate of the *Divine Right of Kings*, which meant that he was responsible for his actions to God and God alone, took some very corporal council. Although Louis' lover for only six years, Jeanne Antoinette Poisson, the Marquise de Pompadour, of common birth, was to be one of his chief foreign policy advisors for over twenty years. Whoever had her ear had the King's as well. No wonder that France's empire was unable to stay the course, no one wanted to take the helm! The *French Disease* (Syphilis) combined with smallpox would bring his dallying and his reign to a painful end. Syphilis, also called the Spanish Disease, was once claimed to have been given to the Conquistadors by the Natives. D.N.A. evidence has proven that this disease existed in Europe long before First Contact.

The Acadians, Métis/Acadians and some of the First Nation peoples, by far not as many of the latter as the two former, sought the security of the French Navy and Fortress Louisbourg on Ile Royale (Cape Breton). Others opted to try new locations on Isle Saint-Jean where the land was of good quality and fish abounded. Still others were making a go of it in the Cape Sable area feeling that they were too small in number to make raiding them a paying proposition. New settlements were set up in Tébok (Chebogue), Abuptic (Argyle), and Chegoggin as late as 1739 hoping that these small settlements would not be as pressured as the more populated centers like Port Royal. I should remind readers that Port Royal did not mean just the town that was renamed Annapolis Royal. The first Port Royal was the *Habitation*, whose replica you can see today at Granville Ferry. As the population expanded outside of its walls, the name Port Royal came to include a much larger area in that vicinity.

When the forts, both French and English, started sprouting up on the Isthmus of Chignecto, options were literally taken out of their hands, the villages around Beaubassin put to the torch by the natives under the control of the priest l'Abbé Jean-Louis Le Loutre. These unfortunates were told to resettle in the *circumcised* parts of Acadia being promised that, eventually, the French would prevail. The French placed particular importance on their relationship with the Mi'kmag, providing them with four missionaries in the 1740's to oversee their allegiance to the *true faith* and those who had brought this *true faith* to them. "In principle, the role of these missionaries was strictly spiritual. In practice, however, religion and national loyalties were impossible to separate. Two of these missionaries, Abbé Jean-Louis Le Loutre and Abbé Pierre Maillard, became deeply involved in political strategies which played the Micmac off against the British – Le Loutre at Shubenacadie and Beaubassin and Maillard on Ile Royale at Port Toulouse (St. Peters) and at Louisbourg."[61]

The British thought that the Mi'kmag were mere putty in the hands of the French missionaries, not realizing that this tribe was fighting primarily for its own existence and its traditional way of life that it saw a strong chance of losing if the English prevailed. Daniel Paul demonstrates that British arrogance in its own right, not the French, was the main reason for their troubles with his people as can be seen in this letter from Lt.-Governor Lawrence Armstrong to Jonathan Belcher dated September 11, 1732: "Our troubles proceed from the influence the French have over the Indians, which will be maintained as long as the English employ the French (Acadians/Métis-Acadians) to sell their goods to the Indians. The French keep us at a distance, make the Indians depend on them, engross the whole management of the fur trade, and run away with the profits. If the French were cut off from these advantages, the profit would go to the Indians, who would thereby be bound to us by the strong ties of self interest."[62] Knowing what sharp traders the British were, one knows where these profits would end up.

The reality of what would probably happen if the King felt surrounded on his chessboard was demonstrated in the European wars when the English, the Dutch, and the Hanoverians tried to chip away at France's frontiers in 1744. Fortunate enough to have an able general in the Maréchal de Saxe, France's home front became stabilized after the Maréchal followed up his great victory at Fontenoy (1745) with other successes which saw France seize Savoy and Nice. "However at the Treaty of Aix-la-Chapelle (1748), France gave back all its conquests, and the *status quo* was restored in India and Canada. The war had been costly in terms of men and money; in fact, it had proved necessary to introduce the *vingtième* (the twentieth part of each person's income) but the tax, which was ill-distributed and unevenly collected, gave rise to much anger, to the point where the phrase *Tu es bête comme la paix* (You're as stupid as peace!) became a common insult at the lower levels of society."[63] The above-mentioned status quo included giving Louisbourg back to France, an action by the British authoritarians that was almost unbelievable to the New Englanders who had made a humongous effort to capture this sentinel of both the Saint Lawrence and the fishing grounds of the east coast and was in essence, their chief competitor! Although life was not always easy in Acadia, it did not look like moving to the *Old Country*, where most Acadians had never been and no longer identified with, was a good option.

Those of our ancestors who lived in *occupied* Acadia had been occupied before and felt that they could weather this storm as long as they stuck to their guns. They had developed an affluent communal society, built around family ties, where people pitched in to do the work that could not be easily accomplished by the individual. House raising for newly weds, barn raising, harvesting or other such activities brought the community together not only to accomplish a good deed but also to celebrate the *joie de vivre* that so aptly symbolized this people. They had sculptured the topography of this area to allow them to drain marshes through the *Aboiteau* (dykes fitted with a sluice gate system that allowed salt water marshes to be drained until it became suitable for farming). A home based economy where gardens, livestock, homespun clothing, and food gathering from the surrounding sea and forests could allow these people to almost live the idyllic lifestyle depicted in their namesake Greek painting of the pastures of *Arcadia*.

An interesting description of an Acadian home in Beaubassin has been handed down to us by a New Englander who was visiting there in the 1730's: "They have but one Room in their Houses besides a Cockloft, Cellar and Sometimes a Closet. Their Bedrooms are made something after the Manner of a Sailor's Cabbin, but boarded all around about the bigness of the Bed, except one little hole on the Foreside, just big enough to crawl into, before which is a Curtain drawn and as a Step to get into it, there Stands a Chest. They have not above 2 or 3 chairs in a house, and those wooden ones, bottom and all. I saw but 2 Muggs among all the French and the lip of one of them was broken down above 2 inches. When they treat you with strong drink they bring it in a large Bason and give you a Porringer to dip it with....The Women's Cloaths are good enough but they look as if they were pitched on with pitchforks, and very often stockings were down at their heels."[64] Even if one takes in the bias of the author, one does see that the life in these communities was not full of stress throughout the 1700's. That a New Englander would be a welcome visitor at this time demonstrates that there were strong trading ties between these competing lifestyles and, if left to themselves, some kind of long term arrangement could have been worked out. There were still many good unsettled areas to placate the land seekers.

The majority of our Métis/Acadian ancestors as well as Acadians of non-aboriginal descent would have continued to evolve as a unique society had not the French clergy and military hierarchy been trying to pull them one way – their way and be damned of the consequences to the common man. The English (especially once Halifax had been founded to offset Louisbourg) military hierarchy, with constant chiding from New England as much as the British Colonial Secretary's Office, continually were seeking an oath of allegiance that would eventually turn them into good little English Protestants once assimilation had been completed. "As early as 1748, British authorities had tried to encourage European Protestants to immigrate to Nova Scotia. Besides French Huguenots who had left France a century earlier, the only other French speaking European Protestants were people from certain areas of Switzerland. Gédéon Delesderniers, a Vaudois of Huguenot origin, came with his family to Halifax in 1749 where he met his nephew Moïse Delesderniers, who was trying with another Swiss from Neuchatel, Abraham Dupasquier, to bring over more Swiss immigrants. Three hundred came to Halifax and then moved on to Lunenburg between 1749 and 1757 – among them francophones such as Pierre Delaroche, a Protestant minister from Geneva, Jacques Laurent and Jean-Pierre Marguerat, both reserve lieutenants....Some of these Swiss were involved in discussions with Acadian leaders, but they were not on the side of the Acadians. In 1755 official allegiance to the British Crown, religious beliefs and personal interests weighed more heavily than common language."[65]

This approach had a negative effect on the Acadians who had been told by former Governor, Richard Philipps, as early as December 1729, that their right to religious self determination, to neutrality in case of war with France or the Mi'kmag, and their right to emigrate would not be abjured with by the *qualified* Oath that he was administering to them. This oath was not sanctioned by the Colonial Office but gave the ruling party a breather while making our ancestors believe that this was, once and for all, a done deal. They also left Governor Philipps in control of Acadia from 1717 up to 1749, when he was eighty-eight years old. Like an absentee landlord, he spent most of his time in London preferring to let Lieutenant-Governors, like Captain John Doucett (non-Acadian), handle the day to day affairs. He had been in the colony and had personally made this deal with the Acadians. The main reason that they believed him and held out for their version of the Oath that he had acceded to was that Philipps remained as overall governor for such a long time after 1729. When Louisbourg was attacked in 1745, although the local population had supplied the fortress with grain and livestock, it did not rush to a call to arms to defend this bastion of French empire. They felt that it was an English and French issue, not a local matter, and the vast majority stayed at home as a demonstration of their neutrality. Many of the residents of the English colonies to the south and many liberal minded people in Great Britain began referring to them as the *Neutral French.*

This term of reference was not to include the First Nation population, especially after their complicity in the raid on the New England troops stationed at Grand Pré. The winter of 1747 saw Colonel Arthur Noble and some 500 New England soldiers billeted at Grand Pré. The French Canadians had a strong force in Beaubassin under Jean-Baptiste Nicolas Roche de Ramsey and the New Englanders had been forewarned of possible attack by local villagers. "On January 21, 240 Quebecers and 20 Indians set out from

*This action, 11 February 1747, resulted in the deaths of 70 soldiers from Massachusetts, including Col. Arthur Noble. One of the precursors to the Deportation, it incensed New Englanders against our people – another nail into the Acadian coffin even though the French and Indian force had been sent from Quebec.*

Beaubassin. They arrived at Grand Pré on February 10, guided by some young Acadians, and attacked the sleeping soldiers. After 36 hours of bloody fighting, the New England troops surrendered and were allowed to withdraw to Annapolis, bringing their dead, among whom were Colonel Noble and five of his officers."[66] This had been a greater disaster than the Battle of Bloody Creek that Saint Castin and his native allies had perpetrated on that woodcutting detail in the Annapolis Valley in 1711. The idea that British Acadia could not stand without a strong military presence was another reason for the founding of fortress Halifax in 1749. More than ever, the New Englanders under Governor William Shirley felt that the Acadian population must be purged from the region. Then along came Charles Lawrence.

# B. Le Grand Dérangement 1755 to 1763.

The governors who ran Acadia/Nova Scotia, Charles Armstrong and Colonel Peregrine Hopson, were make-do-with-the-situation administrators who tried to maintain the status quo, feeling that the time was not right to force Acadian subservience to King George. Mascarene, administrator from 1740 to 1749, wanted to set up mainland Nova Scotia as a buffer zone for New England. However, Governor Armstrong committed suicide and Governor Hopson, former English commander at Louisbourg, fell ill in 1754 and returned home. This left a vacancy that was filled by Charles Lawrence, a military man with military solutions. He was familiar with the 1745 proposal, by the Annapolis Council, to deport the Acadian population. He knew that Governor Edward Cornwallis, founder of Halifax 1749, another military man in the true sense of this term, had also wanted them gone but feared making them leave would only reinforce the French in the next bout of fighting. Lawrence also knew that the British Board of Trade was leery of mobilizing a population of over 13,000 who would, by right, have a great hatred for the people who pried them from their homes, their churches, and the much revered resting places of their ancestors.

Lawrence's chess game was not one of finesse. He was willing to sacrifice as many pieces as were necessary to secure the end-game that after all was over, his king would still be the one standing. The game of chess was all about war and so was Lawrence. In order to beat your enemy, you first had to develop a hatred that would see you through to the end. Although the Board of Trade urged caution and compassion towards the Acadians in the *advice* they sent the Governor in March, 1754, his response showed that his mind was already made up. He stated: "The Acadians had for years been guilty of obstinacy, treachery, partiality to their own Countrymen, and...ingratitude for the favor, indulgence and protection they have at all times so undeservedly received from His Majesty's Government. He was, he said, very far from attempting a step (Deportation) without your Lordship's approbation, yet I cannot help being of opinion that it would be much better, if they refuse the Oaths, that they were away."[67] The guns were loaded, the powder was in the flash pan, and all that was needed now was a spark to fire it up.

This spark was *provided* by Governor Lawrence himself. He convinced Governor William Shirley in Boston that Fort Beauséjour was being prepped to launch an all out attack on Nova Scotia. The New Englanders were tiring of this constant threat to their borders and their fishery so Shirley authorized Robert Moncton and John Winslow to take a force of 2000 men to clear out this threat in the Isthmus of Chignecto. Had Governor Lawrence been absolutely truthful? If one believes that the end justifies the means – yes. Was Fort Beauséjour in any condition to spearhead a serious attack on Halifax and the rest of mainland Nova Scotia? No. They would be hard pressed to withstand a siege and Lawrence knew it. British naval dominance in the Atlantic at this time was unquestionable. King Louis' ministers had mounted an armada consisting of half the French fleet and five seasoned battalions of French soldiers in 1747 under the Duc d'Anville. The gods had not been kind to the commander nor his fleet. North Atlantic gales broke up the fleet and epidemic decimated its ranks, killing almost half the force including the Duc. A similar bout of bad luck would hit the French in 1759 when they attempted to relieve Quebec and Montreal.

Some people believe that bad luck is the result of things beyond your own control. Others believe that you make your own. The English had dealt with the *Divine Right of Kings*, the idea that the whole country must bow to one person's pleasure, when they deposed the Stewarts in 1688. Their monarchy now served at the Parliament's pleasure, the middle class was much more engaged and merit, not so much how close you were related to the monarch, dictated most positions of power. It would be many years and a series of revolutions before France could engage Britain on an equal footing. The constant draining of wealth and manpower by the Bourbons at a rate faster than their country could replenish left the writing on the wall for her colonies as well.

Fort Beauséjour came under attack on 2 June1755. In no condition neither materially nor physically to withstand a prolonged siege, the Commander, Louis du Pont Duchambon de Vergor, capitulated 16 June. Numbers vary but rough estimates place 300-400 Acadians and Métis/Acadians inside Beauséjour and though Duchambon swore that he had forced them to participate under pain of death. Some of our common ancestors in Western Nova Scotia participated inside the fort. Governor Lawrence had his proof that our people would take up arms against England when the occasion presented itself. Things were also heating up in the Ohio Valley where future President George Washington, serving as a British officer, was to suffer his first taste of defeat to the French. Colonel Washington had set up a defensive position, named Fort Necessity, on low ground. The French set up their guns overlooking this fort and pounded it into submission. This demonstrates the difference in training received by colonial militia versus the British army corps.

Acadians in Grand Pré had their weapons seized. Acadian boats were also confiscated. (The Canadian government would do the same thing to Japanese and Chinese citizens during World War II). The main difference here was that war had not even been officially declared against the French, let alone their Acadian descendents, until 18 May1756. In a quandary, the Acadians sent representatives were sent to Halifax twice. Each time they were told to take the unconditional oath. They refused the section that would force them to take up arms and were imprisoned. Charles Lawrence then issued his infamous proclamation to the commanding British officers at Beauséjour, Annapolis, and Piziquid (Windsor) that would forever (or so he thought) seal the fate of the residents of Acadia. I shall, at this time, make full disclosure of this proclamation dated 31 July1755 in Halifax:

Governor Lawrence to Col. Monckton

The deputies of the French inhabitants of the districts of Annapolis, Mines and Piziquid, have been called before the council, and have refused to take the oath of allegiance to his Majesty, and have also declared this to be the sentiments of the whole people, whereupon the council and it is accordingly determined that they shall be removed out of the country as soon as possible, and as to those about the Isthmus who were in arms and therefore entitled to no favor from the government it is determined to begin with **them first;** and for this purpose orders are given for a sufficient number of transports to be sent up the Bay with all possible dispatch for taking them on board, by whom you will receive particular instructions as to the manner of their being disposed of, the places of their destination and every other thing necessary for that purpose.

In the meantime, it will be necessary to keep this measure as secret as possible, as well as to prevent their attempting to escape, as to carry off their cattle etc., and the better to effect this you will endeavor to fall upon some stratagem to get the men, both young and old (especially the heads of families) into your power and detain them till the transports shall arrive, so as that they may be ready to be shipped off; for when this is done it is not much to be feared that the women and children will attempt to go away and carry off the cattle. But least they should, it will not only be very proper to secure all their shallops, boats, canoes and every other vessel you can lay your hands upon; but also to send out parties to all suspected roads and places from time to time, that they may be thereby intercepted. As their whole stock of cattle and corn is forfeited to the crown by their rebellion, and must be secured & apply'd towards a reimbursement of the expense the government will be at in transporting them out of the country, care must be had that nobody make any bargain for purchasing them under any color or pretence whatever; if they do the sale will be void, for the inhabitants have now (since the order in council) no property in them, nor will they be allowed to carry away the least thing but their ready money and household furniture.

The officers commanding the fort Piziquid and the garrison of Annapolis Royal have nearly the same orders in relation to the interior inhabitants. But I am informed those will fall upon the ways and means in spite of all our vigilance to send off their cattle to the island of St. John & Louisbourg (which is now in a starving position) by the way of Tatamagouche. I would therefore, have you without loss of time, send thither a pretty strong detachment to beat up that quarter and to prevent them. You cannot want a guide for conducting the party, as there is not a Frenchman in Chignecto but must perfectly know the road.

Chas. Lawrence"[68]

Although tradition has it that the Deportation began in Grand Pré, as we can see, it actually began in Beauséjour where a strong military body was in place and in control. Technology in the realm of communication being what it was at the time helped the English keep the full extent of their plans secret for a while but once the secret was out mainland Nova Scotia was in a state of crisis for its native inhabitants, aboriginal and non-aboriginal, that was to span the rest of the 1750's carry into the 1760's and for some, especially the aboriginals, has not yet ended. Communities were not only torn apart intentionally. The logistics of such an upheaval created its own set of problems. Once the people were in the know, those who had not been incarcerated due to the subterfuge used by Colonel John Winslow and others like him, took to the forests or delayed their capture by fleeing to Ile Saint Jean (Prince Edward Island) or Louisbourg. During the Deportation if they were captured they were at the mercy of the British and the elements, on shore and out at sea. Many of our relatives perished either in transit or of inhumane treatment as prisoners of war, crammed in places like George's Island at the mouth of Halifax Harbor.

Even those who eluded the British and *their* native allies, eventually the scarcity of food and severe winters drove many to give up to the enemy rather than watch their families fritter away much in the same way that German Concentration Camps were operated (minus the mass executions) during the Second World War. If you think that this is a stretch, check the records to see how many people died prematurely in the run up years before the Deportation, during the Deportation, or as a direct consequence of the Deportation. Further check if you can find anywhere that Governor Lawrence thought that this was a bad thing. Would paying a bounty on scalps help clear out those hard to get places? Scalping bounties may have been instigated by Charles Lawrence on his watch, but they had been enacted by Cornwallis as early as 1749, boosted up to fifty pounds sterling per head on 21 June1750. "The scalping bounties also adversely affected the Acadian population, because many of them were part Mi'kmaq or were related to Mi'kmaq families by marriage. Many Acadians were also scalped by the bounty hunters because they were handy and hated"[69] This preemptive action taken by Cornwallis may have been rescinded later in 1752 and Cornwallis was replaced by Hopson but, overall, Cornwallis was not disgraced nor discharged of his military authority. Was it not he who managed to be **The** military leader in charge of His Majesty's forces in Yorktown, New Jersey, 1780? That action culminated in England's Thirteen Colonies creating their own country, one that was to eventually claim the superiority Britannia had for so long claimed as her own. Lawrence saw that *strong men must make strong choices.* He had at his disposal Captain Goreham, who had not only been in charge of the New England *Rangers* given the job of extermination with his mixed group of *Whites* and American *Indians,* he had also been part of the Halifax council that had *raised the anty* in 1752.

Commandant Preble had been in charge of the first Expulsion in Cape Sable in April, 1756, when he and his detachment apprehended our people from Port Latour, Barrington Passage, Sherose Island, Doctor's Cove and Shag Harbor. "... arrived at Port Latour on the 21st and disembarked 167 soldiers. At night they crossed the (Baccaro) peninsula on foot and surprised the Acadians in their bed. They set fire to 44 buildings. Then they walked the prisoners to the several vessels which were awaiting them at Baccaro Passage. There were 72 in all." http://www.geocities.com/Heartland/Meadows/2700/story31.htm  They were some of the *lucky* ones, ending up in Massachusetts between Plymouth and Gloucester. Shelburne County was down and out in '56. The fall of 1758 was to see much of Yarmouth County put to the torch. This force was under the command of Major Roger Morris, who himself was under the command of Colonel Robert Monckton, had a force of 325 soldiers under his command. This included Captain Joseph Gorham's rangers who did much of the scouting.

East Pubnico, the home of the d'Entremonts, with its Manor house, Church and other buildings was laid waste. What the raiders could not use, they burnt. They did not capture any prisoners here as the people had fled to the interior to escape these English. Morris must have been well piloted for, after clearing the Argyles, they made their way through the Tusket Islands in Schooner Passage, heading for the Landry's and others who had occupied Chebogue in 1739. Again the inhabitants had fled up-river to escape and again the burning and looting began. Gorham made better use of the waterways this time using two whale-boats to go up the Chebogue River where, on Sunday 4 October, he surprised Father Desenclaves and his Chegoggin congregation, 61 souls, at mass. A mother and her six children who were not attending services were also taken. For whatever reason, the priest told Gorham about another 21 Acadian families and six Indian families located up the Tusket River at the head of Lake Vaughn. These families were not caught at home, but there was no such thing as home by the time the soldiers were done. The prisoners of this raid were first transported back to Halifax and were then treated to a winter crossing of the North Atlantic, the survivors touching down in France 16 February1759. http://www.geocities.com/Heartland/Meadows/2700/story32.htm

The second raid had not accomplished all that Charles Lawrence wanted. On 12 October1758, with Louisburg done for, he had began offering the beautifully developed farmlands, the woodlots and other attractants to new settlers, especially from the colonies of New England, New York, Connecticut and Philadelphia where good land was getting harder to find or old land was getting *tired* from over farming. Interested people from these places formed companies and hired agents to come and see if expectations equalled to the sale's pitch. According to Rev. J.R. Campbell, a prominent Yarmouth County historian of the 19th Century, the takers from the *Phillies* were the most interested in Southwestern Nova Scotia. These agents and their clients wanted further clarification from Lawrence, so he issued a second proclamation 11 January1759. The issue of religion is dealt with in some detail so I shall insert it here to show where his heart lay "That as to the article of Religion, all liberty of conscience...is secured to persons of all persuasions, *Papists excepted,* ... Protestants, dissenting from the Church of England, whether they be Calvinists, Lutherans, Quakers, or under what denomination so ever, shall have free liberty of conscience, and may erect and build meeting houses for public worship, and may choose and select ministers for the carrying on Divine service and administration of the sacraments, according to their several opinions...."[70] Not to make himself seen in a bad light, Lawrence knew that he still had the refugees holed up in the wilderness somewhere up the Tusket River whom Gorham had sent a letter *requesting* them to surrender in October1758, before leaving that area.

They had sent him a letter to be delivered to Governor Pownall in Boston, dated Cape Sables 15 September1758. Father Clarence d'Entremont, in his 33rd of 100 Acadian Stories gives us a peek at excerpts from this letter, signed by Joseph Landrey (aided by Charles Dantermong) most likely written in English by merchant associate, Mark Haskell, who saw to it that the letter was delivered. "To His Excellency Thomas Pownall, esq. and Honorable Council of Boston... If it might please your Excellency and Worthy Council to settle us here in this land where we now live we shall ever hold our bounded duty to love and honor you with our last Breath, and... we are heartily willing to do whatever you require... also willing to support and maintain the War against the King of France... We are in all about 40 families which consist of about 150 souls... We beg that if we may no longer stay here that we may be received into New England to live as the other Neutral French do for we had all rather die here than go to any French dominions to live" They had sent their plea to the right preacher but to the wrong church. Pownall, who in the 45 years mainland Acadia had belonged to the English, knew that the people of the Cape Sable region, especially the d'Entremonts, had done much commerce with Boston. However, his Council had the final say and no family in Cape Sable had enough influence to be exempted from being on the wrong side of what they considered to be a just war against the French whom they continually saw as pirates preying out of Louisburg or as raiders with Indian allies looking to kill them all in their sleep.

It is quite possible that Charles Lawrence felt *snubbed* by these "Land ruffians, turned pirates". He painted all peoples of French descent with the same brush so he decided to let the deprivations of another harsh winter further soften them up. He would ask Major Erasmus Philips, stationed at Fort Annapolis, to send in someone to clean up what was left. Who would get this job? You guessed it, Captain Gorham and his rangers. They rounded up 152 souls and had encamped, with virtually no facilities, from the end of June until the 10th November1759, on George's Island. Eight died on the island, four more perished at sea on another winter crossing that saw them in England just before the New Year and in Cherbourg, France a couple of weeks later. I have Goreham friends whose ancestors settled the Wood's Harbor, Barrington and Cape Island area after the Deportation. I wonder how they knew about the good land opportunity.

War against the willing can be a mind-altering sight. War against the unwilling including the elderly, the infirm, women and children has never been palatable to the public at large yet we see it done over and over again in the name of political expediency. Vietnam? Bosnia? Iraq? The big difference back then is that you could eyeball those you were mistreating, make yourself grin and bear it. Not all soldiers felt the same way. Some of them must have been in an awful state, those who had long service in Nova Scotia, who had married into the indigenous population and now had to oversee the destruction of the dreams and aspirations of their in-laws, the blood of their children. To carry out their orders may have broke their hearts but not to have carried out their orders could put them in front of a firing squad. I'm certain that some covert things were done but not very much.

Another factor that is not much brought up is the cost of war and who made the money. In modern times the best way to revive a stagnating economy is to go to war! Like it or lump it, war has a voracious appetite for men and machinery. Soldiers have to eat, be clothed, be provided with the weaponry of war, be transported, and, in case of casualties, be replaced. Money drives all of these factors. Some merchants become very prosperous each time a call-to-arms is made. Who is to pay and who is to be paid was another key factor that brought about the American Revolution or the War of Independence, depending on which side of the fence you were sitting. Is it a wonder that so many old transport vessels foundered and disappeared during this forced evacuation? Why were so many land companies being set up in the New England colonies to come and claim prime real estate in early 1758 before the game of empire was up? Were we just the casualties of war or were we the casualties of economics?

I do not propose to rehash the many trials and ordeals that our people went through between 1755 and 1763 when the *all clear* was sounded and put this atrocity to rest. Reading Henry Wadsworth Longfellow's epic poem **Evangeline** will give you a good flavor for what took place. Some of **our** people never surrendered. Others were deported to Massachusetts, others to Maryland, others to Pennsylvania, others to Connecticut and yet others succeeded in making the Atlantic crossing and were either imprisoned in England or deported to France, I can not call this repatriation because they were no longer Frenchmen. Some became French once again. Not all were satisfied with living the life of a peasant farmer in France in the 1750's and 1760's. These run-up years to the French Revolution saw the average peasant in France still tied to the feudal system that made them subsistent farmers tied to the land and the lords who owned them. Life in Acadia had spoiled them to expect more and want more, for themselves and those who were to follow. Many of our people, seeing that Canada was now out of the question, found that they could be accepted in the Spanish colony of Louisiana or the tropical possessions of the Catholic monarchs. Some of our people, content with the fishing opportunities still available on French soil, removed themselves to the islands of Saint Pierre and Miquelon.

Before leaving this section of the book, it is time to devote some time to one of the French missionaries, already mentioned, who spent almost thirty years as a servant of God amongst the Mi'kmag, the Métis, and the Acadians. Whenever we want to refer to a fighting priest who looked to worldly efforts and military deeds to extend French influence over these peoples of Acadia, the name that jumps to mind is Abbé Jean-Louis Le Loutre, the priest who would burn Acadian settlements to insure that the former occupants would remain on the French side of the Missaguash River. Le Loutre was a man of his times, a man of decisive action who merits what has been written about him in the history books – good or bad. The man rarely found in these books of recorded events was actually his mentor, who in the long run, looked to the survival, the maintained existence of the Mi'kmag in this province.

Fresh from the Seminary of the Society of Foreign Missions in Paris, *Abbé Pierre Maillard*, set foot in 1735 on Cape Breton Island. From there he set out to visit three missions: Maligaoueche (Cape Breton); Malpek (Prince Edward Island); and Chigabenakady (Mainland Nova Scotia). Le Loutre was to take the third mission off his hands in 1738 which partially explains why he was so active in the Isthmus of Chignecto region. Maillard taught the word of God to his parishioners with an amazing amount of success. He had gone the extra yard and had not only learned the Mi'kmag language but had also developed the first complete hieroglyphic system that could transform oral tradition into written word. This had been toyed with by Father Christian Leclercq sixty years earlier in Gaspe but Maillard had it refined to such an extent that a group of hieroglyphics could be formed into a distinct idea that in turn could be given an appropriate phrase in the Mi'kmag tongue.

Abbé Maillard, appointed Vicar General of Ile Royale by the Bishop of Quebec in 1740, could have gone back home with the French after New England took Louisbourg in 1745. Instead he followed the Mi'kmag who fled Cape Breton for Nova Scotia and Quebec. After Louisbourg and Ile Royale were returned to the French in 1748, he was given a safe-conduct pass to return to his original mission by Governor Cornwallis. At this time, Maillard built a new church and presbytery on Chapel Island near the southern end of the Bras D'Or

Lake. The second falling of Louisbourg in 1758 saw the Abbé return to mainland Nova Scotia where he would spend his final four years trying to gear up the Mi'kmag and Métis for survival under an empire, that at its peak, controlled one third of the Earth's population. Peace at any cost, was going to be the price of continued existence. We have in our hands a copy of the peace and friendship treaty concluded between Johnathan Belcher and our Métis ancestor Francois d'Azy Mius, chief of the La Hêve Mi'kmag, on 9 November1761 in Halifax. Abbé Pierre Maillard was one of the signatories of this treaty which is to follow:

Treaty of Peace & Friendship concluded by the honorable Jonathan Belcher Esquire, President of His Majesty's Council & Commander in Chief in around His Majesty's Province of Nova Scotia or Acadia with Francis Mius, Chief of the La Have tribe of Indians at Halifax in the Province of Nova Scotia or Acadia.

I, Francis Mius for myself and the Tribe of La Héve Indians of which I am Chief do acknowledge the jurisdiction and Dominion of His Majesty King George the third over the territories of Nova Scotia or Acadia, and we do make submission to His Majesty in the most unique and solemn manner.

I do promise for myself and my Tribe that I nor They shall not violate any of His Majesty's subjects or their dependents in their settlements already made or to hereafter be made, or in carrying out this commerce or in anything what ever within this the Province of His Lord Majesty or Elsewhere.

And if any unlawful robbery or outrage shall happen to be committed by any of my Tribe, satisfaction and retribution shall be made to the person or persons injured.

That neither I, nor my Tribe shall in any manner entice any of His Lord Majesty's Troops or soldiers to defeat nor in any manner insist in conveying them away but on the contrary will do our utmost to endeavor to bring them back to the company, regiment, fort or garrison to which they shall belong.

That if any quarrel or misunderstanding shall happen between myself and any of my Tribe neither I nor They shall take any private satisfaction but we will apply for redress according to the laws established in His Lord Majesty's Domain.

That all English Prisoners made by myself or my Tribe shall be set at liberty and that we will use our utmost endeavors to prevail on the other Tribes to do the same of any prisoners that happen to be in their hands.

And I do further promise for Myself and my Tribe that we will not either directly or indirectly accuse any of the enemies of his most sainted Majesty King George the third our sovereign or not hold any trades or commerce, traffic, or intercourse among them, but on the contrary will as much as may be in our power, discuss & make known to his Majesty's Government any ill feelings which may be formed or contrived against His Majesty's Subjects. And I do further agree that we will not "Traffic, Barter or Exchange" any Commodities in any manner but with such persons or the management of such Truckhauses as shall be appointed or established by His Majesty's Governor at Lunenburg or elsewhere in Nova Scotia or Acadia.

And for the more effectual security of the due performance of the Treaty of every part thereof I do promise and engage that a generous number of persons of my Tribe which shall not be less in number than two persons shall on or before the 1st day of January 1762 reside at La Have at Lunenburg or at such other places in the Province of Nova Scotia or Acadia or shall be appointed for that purpose by His Majesty's Governor of said Province which Villages shall be exchanged for a like number of my Tribe when permitted.

And all these ongoing particulars and every one of them made with The Honorable Johnathan Belcher, Squire, President of His Majesty's Council & Commander in Chief in and over His Majesty's Province of Nova Scotia or Acadia, I do promise for myself and on behalf of my Tribe that new will most strictly keep and observe in the most solemn manner.

In Witness whereof I have hereunto put my mark and seal at Halifax, in Nova Scotia, this ninth day of November 1761 and in the second year of His Majesty's reign. (Mark of Francis Mius D'azy)

Witness (c. Mallard Provose Missionary of Indians)

I do accept of and agree to all the articles of the foregoing TREATY Faith and Testimony whereof I have signed my name and have certified my seal *to be thereto offered the ninth day of November in the second year of His Majesty's reign and in the year of Our Lord 1761.........Johnathan Belcher.............*

The good Abbé Pierre Maillard continued to ratify marriages and baptisms, perform new marriages and baptisms, was appointed Superior of the Seminary in Quebec (Governor Murray, first English Governor of Quebec, refused to sanction any appointment made in France), and did the best he could for his flock but he returned to his Maker in August 1762. Norman McLeod Rogers in his article *Apostle to the Micmacs*, published in the Dalhousie Review, quotes an eyewitness account of Pierre Maillard's funeral in Halifax; "In August last died Mon. Maillard, a French priest who had the title of Vicar-General of Quebec, and has resided here for some years as a missionary to the French and Indians who stood in so much awe of him that it was judged necessary to allow him a salary from our government (200 pounds)...He was buried in the Churchyard by order of the Lieut. Governor, and his pall was supported by the President of the Council, the Speaker of the House of Assembly and four other gentlemen, and Mr. Wood performed the Office of Burial according to our form in the French, in presence of almost all the gentlemen of Halifax, and a very numerous assembly of French and Indians." This kind of respect was almost unheard of at a time when Roman Catholics were barred from holding office in Britain. Combine this with the countless years that Maillard had faithfully served his native France in the tumultuous see-saw back and forth in Acadia/ Nova Scotia. No matter the nationality, this man's heart was in the right place. Had he lived longer, it is difficult to say how much heartache and suffering Abbé Maillard might have deflected from those whom he served.

Maillard was able to help console people in the Halifax area but, of course, the vast majority of our peoples had been scattered to the seven winds by this time and some were destined to make the best of where they found themselves when the extradition process closed down in 1763. Others remained as detainees at various locations, not knowing where to go or what to do with themselves and their families once their *prison time* was up. People like Joseph *Beausoleil* Broussard took matters into their own hands. Jean Francois Broussard, off the ship L'Oranger from La Rochelle in 1661, married Catherine Richard (Michel & Madeleine Blanchard).They had 10 children who were made of solid stock. Their fourth son, "born Joseph Broussard at Port Royal, in 1702, he went to reside at *Le Cran* (south of Moncton, N.B.) in 1740 and took parts in raids against the English in 1747. Declared an outlaw that same year, he was involved in raids again in 1755 when the French and English forces fought around Beauséjour. He kept fighting in the woods around the Petitcodiac with a small band of Acadians, until his surrender in 1759. Freed from British jail in 1763, he went to Louisiana where his family lived."[71] When opportunity presented itself, the Broussards and company also took a toll on the coastal shipping of British subjects. They fought the good fight using gorilla tactics learned from their Mi'kmag associates and kept it up until they knew they couldn't win after hearing about the fall of Louisbourg. "On 16 November1759 faced with the prospect of starvation and a fast-approaching Canadian winter Joseph, his brother Alexandre, and Jean Basque and Simon Martin delivered a petition to the British at Fort Cumberland, giving up the fight. Jean and Michel Bourg led another group of starving Acadians to the fort a few days later. All of then were sent to Halifax, where they were held until the end of hostilities in 1763. They were not deported, most likely, because there was no shipping available, and because, by now, there was no place to send them – the other English colonies had their fill of Acadians."[72]

I have mentioned earlier that Louisiana belonged to Spain since France had ceded this colony as part of King Louis XIV's folly in beginning the War of the Spanish Succession. One could say that he had just given it to his grandson Phillippe, the new King of Spain, but this one man's whims and vanities had major and lasting effects on many people. Though Spain now owned this colony for the next 40 years, it retained much of its French culture and would continue to do so until another man full of whims and vanities, Napoleon Bonaparte, would have the colony sold to the United States of America. A *France* without French controls, or possibly setting up another Acadia away from the sea in Illinois, brought many Acadians south from Halifax or later back across the Atlantic from the France that so many now found so foreign to them.

The Governor of this French-flavored Spanish colony, Ulloa, knew he did not have a large enough population base to defend his colony or feed ever growing centers like New Orleans so he actively sought Acadians, purebloods or mixed bloods, to come and settle. French Catholics would not be problematic with Spanish Catholics and the land had to be developed. Given the choice to settle on *French* soil in Illinois at your own expense or settle in Louisiana where you could get startup grain, a gun, and tools. Even if you were positioned as a buffer zone between the English, the land that you may be fighting for was your own and the support given here was better than they had gotten from the French in Acadia. There also existed the possibility of dyking (levy) some of the Old Muddy Mississippi to reclaim lowlands similar to old times. Some had tried the equatorial French possession of Saint Dominique, but epidemic decimated their ranks.

*Saint Martinsville Church, Louisiana – first church built by Acadians of Nova Scotia. Photo by Donna (Surette) Messenger*

The Broussards, Joseph *Beausoleil* and Alexandre, his brother also called *Beausoleil*, brought their people to the new promised land of Louisiana and were settled in the Attakapas (Saint Martinsville). There, extensive lands were held on the east side of the Bayou Teche by a retired military officer by the name of Jean Antoine Bernard Dauterive. This man wanted to become a *cattle baron* but did not have the man power to develop such an empire. "In April 1765, Joseph and Alexandre Broussard were among the Acadian representatives who signed a contract with Dauterive, under which he provided each Acadian family with five cows with calves and one bull for each of six consecutive years. At the end of the six years, the Acadians were supposed to return the same number of cows with calves of the same age and kind, and they received initially; the remaining cattle and there increase surviving at the time (to) be divided equally

*Church situated in Paincourtville, Louisiana. Photo taken by Donna (Surette) Messenger.*

between (the) Acadians and (Dauterive)." http://www.carencrohighschool.org/la_studies/ParishSeries/Exile/BroussardLedAcadians.htm

Joseph *Beausoleil* Broussard was recognized by the Spaniards for the military tactician that he was around the same time they signed the above mentioned contract, he was commissioned a Captain in the Louisiana Militia and named Commandant of the Acadians. They were not the first Acadians to come to this territory, nor would they be the last. They had performed a great service for their countrymen, helping over 300 of them to cope and survive at all costs. It is a shame that they never lived long enough to watch their *seed* take in the new lands around Bayou Teche and the Vermillion River. Disease did what the English had been unable to do. Either Yellow Fever or Smallpox sent both brothers back to their Maker within a year or so. The English could have been responsible for one of these diseases, for had not Colonel Jeffrey Amherst, the man whose name replaced Beaubassin village as a sign of gratitude by the New England settlers, told his under officers to give Smallpox infected blankets to the Indians in order that it spread to all *undesirables*. Many Acadians, not given much of a fair shake in the English colonies, were to follow the Broussards to Louisiana. 1766-1770, close to 700 left from Maryland and Pennsylvania to seek a better life. Even Maryland, with its large Roman Catholic population, had not been able to cope with the number of Acadians that had been assigned to them

*Cyprus Lake, situated on the campus of the University of Southwestern Louisiana, Baton Rouge. Photo by Donna (Surette) Messenger.*

A rebellion which included a fair amount of friction between the Spanish and Acadians as to where the latter were to settle may have scared off new settlement for a number of years but in 1785 an agreement between the Acadians who had been duped by Abbé Louis Joseph LeLoutre, the same who had burnt their homes in Beaubassin, into settling on the rock called Belle Isle en Mer. This island off the western coast of Brittany was about as good for farming as Salt Lake, Utah, is for fishing. This feudal colony had run its course by 1772 and the people were spread around the Atlantic ports of France with nothing to do and nowhere to go. After a few years of trying to etch a living in tax starved France, our people greatly warmed up to another chance to create communities away from the ever watchful eye of the monarchy.

The chance came knocking in 1783 under the name of Henri de Péyroux de la Coudrenière, a wheeler and dealer who saw his fortunes rise and fall in Louisiana. He was told by the Spanish that they would help him rise again if he brought enough new settlers to their colony. Married to an Acadian woman, they thought he had considerable influence with them. He didn't. To get the ball rolling, he enlisted the help of an Acadian cobbler in Nantes, Olivier Terrio. People of Acadian descent were solicited from Nantes, Morlaix, Rennes, St. Malo, Caen, La Rochelle, and Cherbourg. First they thought that this would be another wild goose chase like the French Caribbean, Cayenne (French Guiana), or the Falkland Islands which saw those who went either not survive or come back broken and delusional. Eventually they began to warm up to another chance. "On Sunday, 10 May1785, 30 years after the Acadian exile, and after involved negotiations with the Spanish, the first group, 156 Acadians, left King and France for Louisiana. By the end of the year, seven ships had carried more than 1,500 Acadians... to a Louisiana that though Spanish in title was still French in flavor and name."[73]

Another small group of nineteen was brought to the colony by boat from St. Pierre Island, off Newfoundland, by Joseph Gravois just prior to the French Revolution in 1788.

These Cajuns our southern *Petit Cousins* will always be part of our Acadian heritage. They are witness to much more acceptance of racial mixing and racial equality at an earlier stage than we who either stayed or came back. I would like to note that some people from the little Nova Scotian Acadian village of Wedgeport have winter a home on Louisiana's Acadian Coast. Another fact worthy of note is that my younger sister, Donna, took part in an international cultural student exchange program in the early '70's, living and studying for a year at the University of Southwestern Louisiana in Baton Rouge. She, and her late husband, Elden LeBlanc, also of this community, returned to visit and participate in the **Mardi Gras** festivities of New Orleans. They also visited Saint Martinsville and the surrounding vistas, amazed at how much these parishes reminded them of home. Once again, so different but the same!

# Chapter 8.
# The Cats Came Back –
# The Reestablishment of
# Our Peoples in Nova Scotia

## A. Exploring Why the British Became so *Lenient*

Many of our earliest Acadian Ancestors were literate and occupied positions of trust and respect before the Expulsion. Where ever they were dumped during the Expulsion years, their natural attributes, or their French education proved to be a hindrance rather than a plus. The colonies to the south saw us in the same light then as the country they evolved into see the Hispanic influx of today. The sheer numbers of the 21st Century immigrants is going to cause the United States to deal in a much better fashion than the seven or eight thousand forced ÈmigrÈs were given back then. Many colonies did not want to give even the most menial of jobs to our ancestors either out of bigotry, jealousy or fear that whatever was entrusted to them would be stolen. That is why many were not allowed to settle in the most rational locations around the sea where they might hire on and make a living by fishing, something most healthy detainees were capable of doing.

This was a time to stick it to the papists, and stick it they did. It was not bad enough that families had been broken up during the transshipment process. Many people from the Thirteen Colonies saw a chance to get cheap labor. They enticed children away from destitute parents and grand-parents. Those parents, who survived the incarceration and humiliation of the Deportation years, were to be further humiliated and heart-broken when they sought to bring their children back home from exile. By the time they were in any condition to leave, indoctrination, Anglicization, and full bellies had convinced a large number that their lot, even at the bottom of the totem pole, was better than their parents were able to provide them in the early days. Many of our people living in the United States of America today had their names changed from Le Blanc to White, Le Jeune to Young, Brun to Brown, or else, like the Black American slaves, were given the name of their owner. Though the vast majority has been assimilated into the American mosaic, there may be some out there looking for their roots, either for genetic reasons or, like most of us, simply wanting to know. May the advertising of the 2004 World Acadian Congress arouse their interest?

Be that as it may, by 1764 most of North America now was part of the British Empire and King George III's royal ministers knew that any serious threat, perceived or real, from the pre-Expulsion Maritimes no longer existed. These former residents were given permission to return, if indeed they had left, or were removed from the stockades from Fort Cumberland, George's Island, and Cape Breton, to resettle. Two stipulations, of course were to be made first. Number one goes almost without saying; they must swear the *Long Oath of Allegiance* forever making them British subjects. This did not make them *full* subjects for they, as long as they were practicing Catholics, were unable to hold public office in Nova Scotia. That was only rescinded in 1830, three years before Britain abolished slavery in her Empire. In 1766 the ordinance prohibiting Catholics from owning land was removed from the books. The Oath of Allegiance was removed from the province in 1827. What remained on the books was stipulation two. Acadians, Métis/Acadians and whoever else lost their lands, livestock and whatever other possessions left behind during the Expulsion were no longer to consider these lands or items redeemable.

The first group of primarily New England Planters had been invited over to take what they wanted, the main sales pitch having been the lands already under cultivation. They were slated to be the backbone of this new Province of Nova Scotia and nothing was to be put in their way. Many people that I have spoken with over the years thought that the term Planters referred to people who had moved from the Plantation Colonies but it doesn't. It is simply an Elizabethan term for colonists or settlers. So, in the beginning, on paper there did not seem to be that much of a disparity between these new settlers and the old settlers who had been ripped from their lands. Nothing could be further from the truth. Holding to the Roman Catholic faith, forced to return and resettle in little groups, with most of your previously acquired fortune either lost, stolen or hidden in areas where you could not reclaim it under pain of death all make for a tailor made lower class, ready to do almost anything for whatever the hirer is giving, became a byline for the returnees. Other new settlers were quickly grabbing up property in Nova Scotia. They came from the British Isles (mostly excluding the Catholic Irish of southern Eire), Germany, France and Switzerland.

The intrigues that brought about the American Revolution/War of Independence almost saw our New England Planters, who were two thirds of Nova Scotia's population when it began in 1775, make us the *Fourteenth Colony.* British naval superiority and the huge military force at Halifax more than likely saved the day. This war brought another cultural shock to our people when the United Empire Loyalists began showing up on our shores in 1784. It looked for a while as if these settlers, who were mostly well-off in the new United States and had given up much for *Crown and Country,* now expected Crown and Country to repay their sacrifices. They took a good look at Shelburne. Some stayed, exploring opportunities in lumber, shipbuilding and fishing enterprises but many found the land to be much inferior to what they had become accustomed to. The Saint John River, both estuary and valley, looked much more suitable to perhaps rekindle their little North American aristocracy, more and more gravitated across the Bay of Fundy. So many Loyalists settled there that by 1784, their more conservative views being at odds with the more liberal views of the Planters, a petition of separation was requested and granted, dividing Nova Scotia into two distinctive colonies: New Brunswick and Nova Scotia. Did this split help our cause any? No. It just provided Métis groups in two provinces with more bureaucracy to overcome.

## B. The Silent Years.

Education has been noted earlier. As our people came back after 1766, especially if they settled in small villages where manual labor took precedence over mental labor, a lot of their education or even want to self educate was lost. Petitions to the provincial government became more difficult to deliver if you had to go through an English surrogate who might *doctor* the document if it was in conflict with his own lifestyle. Priests, when available, filled in the void but this also enhanced their corporal powers to make their spiritual edicts more palatable. Remember, a deal had been struck in Quebec, between Britain's Governor Murray and the Bishop of Quebec that would have major implications here. Quebec was looking to survive with a large French Canadian population that it would be impracticable to rule, at that time under the British systems of laws and taboos. Murray, like his replacement Guy Carleton, felt that these people would stand a better chance of becoming good British subjects if they were allowed to keep their legal system with regards to civil matters and their religious system intact including *la dime* (church tithes/taxes) for the time being. The British criminal system was more lenient than its French counterpart so it was an easy sell. Looking at what was brewing in the south probably had a sobering effect on these governors also. By placating the French Canadians, a strong source of supply and reinforcement was plucked from the hands of the Americans and helped Britain retain a sizeable portion of its North American empire. We, of course, were not offered the same deal. The Bishop would keep our people quiet by sending a majority of Irish priests who could not speak French, but could keep the new little flocks in line. And so it came to pass. If silence is golden, we became a very golden folk.

Our aboriginal ancestors were even in a worse plight. A chief of the Ottawa, named Pontiac upset British plans by beginning a major rebellion in the west, capturing all forts in that general area except Detroit. Although this rebellion only lasted a few months, many lives were lost and fear of renewed Indian attacks were everywhere. The Proclamation of 1763 was supposed to set up parts of Quebec and modern day Ontario as well as all lands west of the Allegheny Mountains into an *Indian Empire* where First Nation peoples could regain their old life of hunting, fur trading and following the food without worrying about non native interference. This, of course, got the southern colonies howling mad because it essentially cut them out of the fur trade and the acquisition of new lands for settlement, which they all thought, in the fashion of Daniel Boone, was their God given right. It is amazing how so many cultures, caught in a two sided rivalry, pray to the same God, no matter what name they give Him, expecting him to take sides to the detriment of the other.

The British wanted to keep a strong military presence in these colonies to keep the natives in check. The home government would carry two thirds of the cost but they wanted the colonies to pay one third – to be collected in the form of taxation. People liked taxes then as much as they do now. A more representative governmental society was sprouting up in the thirteen southern colonies and they began using the old *No Taxation without Representation* ruse. This played well, especially in New England, where entrepreneurs were setting up rival shipping companies to compete directly with the mother country. Unrest here probably spurred on those of our ancestors who had lingered a bit before either heading back home or south to Spanish Louisiana. Pontiac, like many aboriginals in Nova Scotia, had hoped that the King of France had merely taken a hiatus but would come back with all of his military might and glory to reclaim their lands for them and set things up the way they were before. They wished the same wish but got the same result. The Mi'kmaq were told they could hunt and fish and gather where they wanted in the hinterland of Nova Scotia. What they were not told was that this only applied as long no non native settlers decided to settle any given area.

Squeezed, bit by bit, off their lands and corralled into reservations, many of our aboriginal brothers still await their day of reckoning. Disease and malnutrition further diminished their numbers to the point that these *basket weavers* were considered more of a nuisance than a threat.

It was in this backdrop that our people began returning *wholeheartedly* around 1766. Some decided to stay in eastern Quebec where they were absorbed into the French Canadian landscape. The Moncton, Shediac, Cocagne, Memramcook portion of southern New Brunswick became home for a large Acadian population. Some settle in the Grand Sault, Madawaska region along the New Brunswick/Maine border. Yet others settle on the north coast around Bathurst, Caraquet and Beldune, away from their old stomping grounds. As a student at l'Université de Moncton in 1968, I vividly remember people from this last place feel like they said it all when, exclaiming their home grounds would say: *I'm from the North Shore and Dats for Shore!* Prince Edward Island saw some return, settling in Rustico and Mont Carmel for the most part. The Magdeleine Islands, owned by Quebec, has a number of Acadian and Métis/Acadian families. My Great-Grandfather, Alexandre Boudreau, sailed into these islands a single man but came home with a bride, Melanie Deveau.

Nova Scotia has many of our people in her midst. Chezzecook was probably the first area settled by Acadians once the *gates* to George's Island were opened in 1663. In the 1760's whores, a sanctioned necessity where thousands of naval and military men looking to *let off steam* are lodged, were treated much better than our people so they looked to leave as soon as was conveniently possible. Some remained in Chezzecook; others used it as a staging place from where they could send representatives to find them new lands. Cheticamp, on Cape Breton Island, was settled by fourteen families in 1782. Nicolas Deny's earlier encampments were settled on this Island also. Isle Madame and the coastal communities from Arichat to L'Ardoise and Saint Pierre make up an area that was built up as much by the Protestant Robbins family business's need for manpower as anything else. The north eastern mainland villages of Pomquet, Tracadie, Havre Boucher, Larry's River, Charlo's Cove and Port Felix bristle with a who's who of Acadian and Métis/Acadian names, though many of them like those in the more urban centers, like Halifax, have *perdu la langue* (lost their French speaking skills).

I let the cat out of the bag when I stated that Joseph Dugas was the first person to settle in L'Anse des LeBlanc in Saint Bernard District of Clare, Digby County in September, 1768. He was to open the floodgates to Acadian resettlement in this district, the most Acadian district in Nova Scotia today. This minor population explosion of returning French speaking Roman Catholics is why the Reverend Abbé Jean Mandé Sigogne, born in Tours, France in 1760, came here via England to take care of the seven parishes that had quickly developed a need for pastoral guidance between Annapolis and Pubnico. Abbé Sigogne, quitting France due to the excesses of the French Revolution that wanted priests to swear fidelity to the State before the Church, became a pillar of power, both secular and religious, for his adopted people. He served them faithfully as

*Université Ste. Anne and their Church at Church Point, Digby County. One of the key building blocks to put the people of Acadian descent on an equal footing with other ethnic groups in this part of Nova Scotia.*

they served him faithfully until his death, 9 November 1844. There would be no Université Saint Anne in Church Point without the *push,* mentioned earlier, that this man gave to some of our people to reignite the flame of education in Acadia.

Other pioneer families that took up residence *Par en Haut* include: Amirault, Belliveau, Blinn, Boudreau, Comeau, Deveau, Doucet, Gaudet, Jeddry, LeBlanc, Lombard, Maillet, Melanson, Muise, Pothier, Robichaud, Saulnier, Theriault, Thibault, Thibodeau, and Thimot. This municipal unit is the only one in Nova Scotia to operate its day to day business in French. The back to back communities that extend from Salmon River to Saint Bernard provide a main street of many kilometers where everybody knows your name and probably your business too. Métis/Acadians permeate these communities and those like Hectanooga, Corberrie and Concession

*A.F. Theriault Shipyard, Meteghen River, Clare. The largest boat construction and refitting company in our community, this shipyard employs well over 100 people and is used by both the private and government sectors.*

in the Clare interior. A special Métis/ Acadian fishing community is Cape Ste Marie where the Doucet abound. At the time of this publication, Melbourne Muise, a Métis brother whose heart was in the right place, was going to share his experience and sweat lodge with a number of us but the Creator claimed him back first. His longtime friend and companion, Aurel Comeau, was able to pass on the knowledge and usage of the Sweat Lodge of Lac Des Robicheaud to The Eastern Woodland Métis Nation. I will digress from looking at the other communities and families for a minute to pass some of this knowledge on to you.

Lac Des Robicheaud (Wentworth Lake) is the largest lake in Clare, dotted here and there with sixteen islands. It is upon one of these islands that our Lodge is located. You have to portage one island to get to the water passage which brings you to this spot. The Keeper of the Flame goes first to prepare for other participants. The outside fire takes two hours to heat up the *Grandfathers* (porous beach stones). Up to twenty stones may be used in one ceremony. There is an invitation drum located 100 yards from the passage that is sounded by the other members and guests requesting permission to participate in the day's proceedings. They only advance when the come ahead is sounded by the Keeper on his own drum. These drums are constructed of untanned deer hide stretched over a cedar frame when the hide is wet. Lashed tightly together with deer hide lashings, the drum is allowed to dry near a fire or under the sun. Dampness causes the drum to lose some of its sound quality so, before using, it is *dried* to taste, almost like tuning a guitar. In older times, these drums, as was the exterior of the lodge, were made of caribou or moose hide. The accompanying photographs show that our lodge is wrapped with waterproof duck canvas. There are exactly thirteen ribs that the outer covering is wrapped around. This is done to mimic the thirteen moons that cross Mother Earth each year.

The entrance is always on the east side to coincide with the rising sun. You enter to the left and go around the different points of the compass until filled to capacity (6-8 persons). East signifies wisdom and has as its totem the Eagle *Kitpu*. South signifies compassion in life and is symbolized by the Wolf, *Moumouche,* or the beaver, *Kopit,* as is used in this lodge. West is known for its power, the direction of youth, and has for its totem the Bear, *Muin.* North recognizes purity, the balance between good and evil. The Owl, *Gougougueche,* protects this last cardinal point of the compass, completing the circle. Before entering, the fire keeper inserts three to five red hot *Grandfathers* in the interior fire pit. The number used depends upon the special occasion or event that has brought the group together. Smudging or purification, with the smoke of sweet grass, is performed by all individuals before entering the lodge. Participants are then requested to enter, invoking all of our ancestors, after which a deer skin is put in place to cover the opening. Offerings of tobacco or sweet grass are placed on the red hot stones as a gift to the ancestors, followed by water to create the cleansing vapor (steam).

Once the participants have acclimatized themselves to this environment, the lower you remain, the less cumbersome the steam, the Master of Ceremonies begins the process of initiating a spiritual rapport with the animals of this area. One member invoked the spirit of the Mouse, calling to our attention the important role that this little rodent plays in our environment. After invoking the totem, he may speak to whatever issue he is concerned with, either loud enough that the others may hear or in a lower more personal voice. The same exercise is performed by the other occupants, beginning with the member seated nearest to the southern point of the compass. Once everyone has had their say, any other participant may begin the next round of convocations and themes relevant to them as the spiritual cleansing process continues, lasting, at times for many hours.

*Grandfathers* are brought in, always in groups of three to five, to maintain the sweat that cleanses the inner soul as well as the outer body. People entering or leaving must invoke the memories of all our ancestors. The process is complete when all members are satisfied that their needs have been met. Some people may call this activity *nonsense* or might fear that it is leading members of the established religions astray. Actually, just the opposite is true. You partake in a ceremony that brings you closer to your basic religious beliefs, making you take the time, that we often state we just can't find, to reflect on the good things that God has put on this planet for us. If, at the same time, it gives you a better understanding of how you and your own needs fit into this universe, you become a more productive and self satisfied individual. You will find yourself better geared to take on the many challenges of our ever changing environment without going through stressful and expensive sessions with psychiatrists or other medical professionals who, in this country, are already worked to the bone. The last day that we were returning on the lake, two Bald Eagles gave us a *fly by*. That is a sign that all is well in our world. With this in mind, we now go back to the story of our people.

*Deputy Captain of the Hunt, Donald LeBlanc,*
*next to our Sweat Lodge.*

*Last passage to Sweat Lodge.*

*Aurel Comeau, Keeper of the Fire.*

*Some of the "Grandfathers"*

The District of Argyle, in Yarmouth County, is in the heart of the former Cape Sable of Old Acadia. The Planters had ample opportunity to pick the portions of this district that they wanted. "Apart from the land that was granted in 1771 to Benoni d'Entremont and 17 others at Pubnico, all the rest of the present district of Argyle had been granted, either to immigrants from New England or in large tracts to Ronald McKinnon, Ebenezer Moulton and the Reverend John Breynton. As these could not possible fulfill all the obligations of the grants within the specified time limit, they were willing to sell part or all of their holdings at a minimal price to willing settlers, or at least have settlers on them."[74] The d'Entremonts had been fortunate enough that, now the Expulsion issue had been dealt with, they still had associates pre 1755 who thought well enough of them to intercede on their behalf so that the three family heads Joseph, Paul, and Benoni d'Entremont, along with Abel (Tibel) Duon, Jacques and Ange (Archangel) Amirault, Charles Belliveau, Philip Brown, Walter Larkin, Benjamin Sealy, Petitiah Goodwin and seven others, received their *Licenses of Occupation* in November 1771, allowed to

*The Pointe a Rocco site in Ste Anne du Ruisseau where the first chapel was constructed, 1784, to provide services for the returning Acadians and their relatives in Cape Sable.*

chose much of the east side and all of the west side of Pubnico Harbor. It is for this reason that Pubnico has the distinction of being the oldest community still Acadian since 1653. It probably did not hurt to have so many English speaking partners either.

Other Acadian communities with a strong Métis flavor are: Ste. Anne du Ruisseau (Eel Brook), la Butte d'Amirault, l'Isle des Surette, Sluice Point, Hubbard's Point, Wedgeport, la Butte des Comeau, la Pointe des Pickney, Belleville, Springhaven, and Quinan. If anyone was to ask me to label any of these communities in the District of Argyle, I would state, without hesitation, that Saint Anne du Ruisseau is the soul of our Métis/Acadian community. This is where the first of our chapels was built at *La Pointe a Rocco in 1784.* This is where the early post Expulsion families first congregated to hear the word of God, to ratify marriages, to baptize newborns and to pray for the deceased. The *heart,* without a doubt, can be found in Quinan, the Forks or whatever name you want to give it. Named by a grateful Parrish after a Priest

who cared, Quinan is where you still can find the largest concentration of Métis/Acadians who do so many things the old way. Many of our food gathering techniques and grounds are found emanating from this community. If you want to take part in a trap line, go there. If you want to boil down some maple syrup, go there. If you want to hunt wild game, no matter if it is porcupine, rabbit, partridge, deer, or black bear, go there. The skills are still sharp and the people are still willing. They can tell you how to find the herbs and medicines that were in use before doctors could or would visit this inland community and before the automobile could take them out to medical facilities. *L'herbe du saint* (wild sage), *le baume de champs* (wild mint), *la racine noir*

*Ste Anne du Ruisseau Church, Parrish, founded by Père Sigogne with the assistance of Pierre LeBlanc, brothers Pierre and Louis Mius, and Pierre Surette.*

(black root), *le tabac* (ceremonial tobacco), *l'herbe de Saint Jean* (ginger) and other such medicines exist in a natural state, there for the taking if you know what it looks like.

For many years, there was a stage coach/ox cart route that cut through the forest to link the Mius's of Quinan with the Mius-d'Entremonts in Pubnico. This road leaves the main road of Quinan, passing next to the *Club des Audacieux*/Quinan Social Club and comes out at Pubnico Head. Several very old foundations can be found along this road, where homesteads existed over 150 years ago. Painstaking work had been done to remove the rocks from this road. The rocks were used to make stone walls on either side. Some people had to really tough it out inland where the roads were either logging trails or hunting trails learned from the original Mi'kmag occupants of the Forks. One lady, alone in the bush, delivered herself of a dead baby, buried the remains under an oak tree not far from Meshpok Lake. She had to the trauma of digging up the remains so that the authorities, who had gained knowledge of this incident, could rule out foul play.

A portion of the community that maintained Mi'kmag families like the Pictou and the Alexis was called *Cabino*. There are several camps found, using the old coach route, that literally come alive with hunters from the beginning of deer season until rabbit season ends. No new vehicles should be *broken in* on this *road* because you may end up with more breaks than you want. Off terrain vehicles have replaced walking for some but not all. After a heavy snow fall the only way to attempt this route is with snowshoes, skis, or a snowmobile. The Tusket River system has an old dam on the northern end of Meshpok Lake (The place of many rabbits). Many of the lakes and roads in this vast inland region that make up this system maintain their Mi'kmag names to this day. Some, like Bill White's road are named after Métis/Acadians who anglicized their names (LeBlanc/White) to become more accepted amongst the English population.

Some of the Acadian surnames found in the Municipality of Argyle include: Amirault, Babin, Belliveau, Boucher, Boudreau, Bourque, Corporon, Cottreau, d'Entremont, d'Eon, Deveau, Doucet(te), Dulong, Jacquard, Landry, LeBlanc, Moulaison, Muise, Pothier, Surette, Richard, Vacon. Concentrations of certain family names are found where that family may have been a founder or co-founder of one or more of these communities. Tusket, the municipal seat, also has a number of these families as residents.

I have mentioned many communities that are considered Acadian, not Métis/Acadian, in this province because that is what they are. Métis/Acadians live in these villages but do not possess one particular village that we can call our own. No distinction was made at the time of Expulsion and, those who came back knew they were bad enough being french speaking Roman Catholics in an area where the English speaking majority held the purse strings and the political power. Purse strings are further highlighted when one thinks of the following stories. A Planter working the fields that he had *acquired* from the Acadians in the Chebogue settlement stumbled upon a sum of gold that kept his family happy for a number of years. A descendent of the Boudreau family once told me that the Boudreau gold was located under the 101 Highway in a certain spot in the Annapolis Valley. The d'Entremonts supposedly had hidden their valuables on an island in *La Baie des Chicanne*, the body of water that separates Wedgeport from Comeau's Hill. One must remember that the high value placed on pelts at that time means that some of the *treasure* could have been of a perishable nature that, after a number of years, would disintegrate. The same holds true for any paper money received in payment made to them from the British outposts prior to the Expulsion. Many never came back to reclaim their goods because they were either dead or dared not get caught on properties that were no longer theirs, looking for items that the government in Halifax had told them they were forfeit if it had not gone with them at time of forced removal.

Always a sociable people amongst themselves, the Acadians and their Métis/Acadian relatives contented themselves with settling their small communities, as per directives, claiming what they could from the soil and Mother Nature and hiring themselves out to sea to whomever would take them. Once again, in the beginning, most of the ship owners were English speaking gentlemen looking to make the most off their investment by employing at the lowest wage possible. No self respecting person was about to heap further scorn and misery on himself or his family by making it well known that he was part aboriginal, especially as they saw how hard their aboriginal relatives were faring. Even to this day, the stigma and paranoia associated with this perceived *stain* on their family tree has some Métis/Acadians, especially the older ones, renouncing their heritage to this day. I have an aunt who says that she would rather say that she had black blood rather than Indian blood, this a woman who worked in the United States throughout the terrible times that African Americans faced in the 50's, 60's and in some instances to this very day. I do not in any way want Americans of this ethnic group to feel that we over here do not know of the pain and suffering that their forced participation in the first three centuries of the American Dream went through. We have Canadians with the same background over here. I refer to the difficulties and obstacles overcome in the second half of the 20th Century to make a point.

## C. Keeping the Old Ways Going in Modern Times

As much as possible, in the early days of resettlement, the barter system was used almost exclusively amongst our people. People exchanged goods and services, establishing a barter price for each item. For example, the miller could exchange sawed lumber for livestock, fish, or vegetables with the *cost* being determined in running board feet. Planking was being used not only for housing but also for the construction of boats to chase the herring and other fish off shore. We have a variety of harvestable trees: spruce, fir, beech, hemlock, maple, pine, oak, and hackmatack that would not only satisfy local needs. Trees and lumber became a tradable commodity to the outside world for products not available

*Older gentlemen at the Kayak (Gasperaux) Brook , S.A.R., whose dipping days are done yet they still come to watch and tell stories of yesteryear.*

*A Métis/Acadian dipper – his turn. Most years there are so many Kayaks's to go around that the participants take turns dipping and by the end of the day, everyone goes home satisfied. This has changed from a food fishery to a commercial lobster bait fishery. 2004 was not a good year.*

in this part of the country or, if you were lucky, an amount of hard cash you could save for a *rainy day*. Tree lot management and harvesting are still an important resource, especially in Clare where you may find commercial and family woodlots side by side. Many a retired person still takes great pride in going on his woodlot, usually with a companion or two, to cut his firewood for the next winter or earn an extra income by selling their prime produce. They do not drive themselves like they used to. They enter the woods with their tractor early in the morning and work until a little past noon when they have a bit of refreshment, a lunch, and pack it in, chuckling that they must leave some for tomorrow..

The taxman has become king in our democracy today. The Beatle tune, *The Taxman*, refers to him taxing the pennies placed on a dead man's eyes (the suspicion covered here is that you will need the coins to pass through Hell's gate). For some, especially the overburdened middle class, there appears to be a ring of truth in that statement. Money and the ramifications of *being caught* trading labor or services for *in kind* returns, have made many communities unwilling to chip in and help one another unless you are protected under the umbrella of a *not for profit* society. Once upon a time, when I was a teenager, if a young couple in the community wanted to build a house, there was never a lack of willing hands to help pour a basement foundation for the cost of refreshments at the end of the job. The same held true for the wall raising or other labor intensive activities. As younger members, we felt that our turn would come somewhere down the line or, if not, the learning experience would be beneficial someday. We still help each other out, but not to the extent that our ancestors did for fear of being labeled part of *the black market* economy. May the mighty dollar and its caretaker not swallow us up in the end!

Other things at that time could be traded for outside products like cotton (to be made into fish nets), iron (to be taken by the blacksmith and made into ploughshares, axes, and other iron implements), or maybe something sweet like molasses. The original outside trading was done with coastal traders who would come in, bargain with the locals for lumber, fish or cattle, and then move their ship on to the next coastal community to repeat the process. When they had a full load, they might bring their cargo down to the West Indies, cut their best deal with the locals there, and when all was done return to Boston, having made money at both ends. Eventually as our communities became more developed, coastal traders were constructed and put into the coastal trade by our own people. These boats usually took two seasons to build, the first season to get the wood during the winter months, let it season, and the following year the actual construction would take place. Communal boats were built with sixteen shares allotted to the sixteen people who provided both the lumber and the manpower to construct a vessel. The only paid member of the work crew was the master carpenter in charge of the project. One of the most successful coastal trading companies found in this area was owned by the J. H. Porter (Pothier) & Co. of Wedgeport. From their huge wharf, extending out from the Wedgeport Cape, Jeremy, followed by his sons Aselmne O. and André, traded successfully with various ports of the World, owning many ships and having shares in many others.

Early fishing was not just done from plank boats either. The Mi'kmag had shown our people how to make fish traps, or weirs, by driving stakes made from spruce into a large circle on the mudflats at low tide, interlacing them with fir, leaving an opening for the fish, mostly herring and mackerel, to enter on the flood tide. For some reason, once fish begin swimming in a circle they continue to do so. As the tide recedes a goodly number of fish remain in the weir and can then be harvested with an oxcart afterwards. Eels were also caught the Mi'kmag way by placing a funnel shaped trap with openings at both ends along the side of sluices or brooks. Frank Pothier, local author, in his booklet on the Acadians of Southwestern Nova Scotia, published 1957, had the following to say about how eeling was carried out in Eel Brook and vicinity. "The eeling season was in the spring and fall. The eels when caught were dumped in holes made on the banks of the brooks. When these holes or dugouts were filled the older people would gather around with their baskets for an equal share of eels. By an agreement the Indians had to be notified, as they claimed a share in the eel catches. A shot was fired from a muzzle loader as a signal and if there was a reply by another shot on the part of the Indians, a certain amount of eels was left for them....After a few years a sense of mutual trust was created between both groups, they learned to live as good neighbors, even a few of one group marrying into the other group. Unfortunately, an epidemic broke out among the Indians which took toll most of the tribe. The survivors decamped, leaving much of their provisions behind as, according to their belief, the evil spirit had taken possession of their encampment and belongings."[75]

Another custom held sacred to our older generations had to do with how a woman took care of one particular member of their livestock – her pig! A source of pride and accomplishment was credited to the wife, by her husband and other members of the community, depending upon how large her pig had grown prior to the slaughtering season in the fall. The woman with the largest pig held status in the community and was the envy of the other housewives who would try their best to figure how to push a porker's weight up and over the 500 pound range. In my own childhood in Wedgeport, there were still a number of subsistence farmers who raised pigs the old way, filling the *slop bucket* with table leftovers, unused milk products, corn husks, and just the right amount of grain as it got close to harvesting time. Harvesting time meant, then as it does now, the proper phase of the moon and other such *requirements* had to be in place before the pig had her day in the shed. Very little of this animal was wasted. Blood pudding was made from, what else, the blood. The head was used for minced meats, pig's feet was a delicacy, the liver and heart were eaten as were the various pork steaks, hams and bacon prepared and consumed over the long winter.

Our people tended to have large families. Contraception was unheard of and, God's will be done, every two years or so a new mouth to feed arrived. As the family grew, chores were shared around the farm and the older children literally raised the younger ones. The lands being not very arable and the chances of practicing crop rotation limited, wild game (waterfowl, rabbits, caribou, moose etc.) was an important staple that seemed to be slipping away as the various communities, French and English, reclaimed their habitat.

An author must strive to remain within his element when wishing to relate stories of his natural environment. How he views the bounty given to us by our Divine Creator and how he makes use of these natural resources may vary between himself and others in his community. Most of my food gathering experiences have been as a collector of various berries from the forest; clams and mussels from the ocean; and the odd lobster for personal consumption. I have fished for smelts, mackerel, bluefish, cod, haddock, halibut, trout and salmon when these species presented themselves and were not an endangered species. As a young boy of fourteen, along with fellow Métis/Acadians, I would borrow a shotgun from an Elder, purchase rounds of ammunition at five cents a round from the local Co-op Store (mid 1960's), and head to the woods to run a trap line for rabbits as well as hunt these creatures or other small game like partridge, grouse, or pheasant.

*Successful goose hunt in the Tusket Islands using observation, stealth, and concealment – the old ways, rather than the much commercialized and overpriced decoy system. Métis/Acadian hunters Roland Surette, Donnie Jacquard, Carl d'Entremont, and Anthony Pothier. Photo by Rhoda Jacquard.*

The earlier and colder winters back then made it possible for us to cross the northern frozen portion of Goose Bay (Baie des Chicanne) so that we could hunt the more lucrative grounds on the eastern shore of Comeau's Hill. Duck hunting, especially Black Ducks, Green Winged Teal, Blue Bills, and the odd Canada Geese enticed us to take selective shots, as often we could only afford two or three rounds a hunt. If you missed one duck, you did not compound this error by trying another *Hail Mary* shot at the same duck. The stoicism passed down to us by our ancestors made us realize that if not successful today, another day would present itself – perhaps with a better outcome. As we progressed in age, the size of the beasts hunted increased. Deer are at the top of the wildlife list harvested by our community. From the elders, we learned the various methods of hunting this animal. In Wedgeport, Comeau's Hill, on the Black Pond Road, on Saint Martin's Island, Wilson's Island and a number of other special places, we were shown how to hunt the land. This meant where the best funneling (interception), feeding or sleeping areas could be found. We were also taught how to incorporate the winds into the hunt, how they were used by the deer and when the best times to hunt certain areas during prevailing winds.

The Elders taught us how to still hunt, how to stalk, how to make use of tree stands, and the safest way to carry our rifles or bows. The masking of scent did not necessitate running out to the store to buy the fancy new lures. Most things were kept simple and, although many men feel the urge to hunt alone, we were often counseled to hunt in groups of two to four, depending on whether you wanted to *run* certain areas to drive out deer to a designated shooter or not. This meant that help was never far away and the task of harvesting a successful hunt could be prepared much more effectively. Many times, especially if one of the Elders was with you, the work at preparing the animals would be combined with stories from the past and hints on how to complete the job at hand so that the meat would get home in a clean and edible condition. The most important part of the hunt is this last part.

The exchange of stories around a campfire or in a hunting lodge provides all participants with a chance at being one with nature while having an opportunity to listen to others and learn. One of the things that we have learned early as Métis/Acadians in Southwestern Nova is that taking of all life is sacred. Taking a minute or two to thank the Creator through the animal that you have just harvested is an excellent method of giving thanks for your own continued existence. Like all living things, we are aware (even if not fully) when we are born. Sometimes we even know why. What we do not know is precisely when we are to die. That is our mortality and the mortality of all living things, from the ameba to the whale. The sounds of nature that you hear in the wilderness at night all have a purpose, no matter how eerie they may seem. Many a hunter, including this author, has had a better chance of pondering the purpose of the universe on a clear starry night. Over the millennium, it is good to know that our ancestors have done the same thing. The same as the rest of us, with the exception of people like Issac Newton, Albert Einstein, Stephen Hawking, they did not come up with concrete answers. The answers they did come up with provided for the continued existence of their blood lines over what seem like many years for mankind, yet form just a blink in the eye by Mother Earth.

I had a delightful round table conversation, the first day of spring this year, with Eulalie Doucette, a lady still living by herself in her own home in Quinan during her *Golden Years*. Her late husband, Nelson (Benoit), had served with

*Métis/Acadian men in Quinan getting together to saw their own lumber in the 1930's.*

the Black Watch Regiment in World War II, and had lived firsthand the horrors of war. At the table with us were two of their sons, Edward and George, and another Métis/Acadian, Reginald (Reg) LeBlanc of South Ohio. The purpose for this discussion was to discuss food gathering techniques used by the Métis/Acadians around the turn of the 20th Century up into the 1960's. Eulalie had not only lived some of the experiences we are about to explore, her Father, Pierre (Pierrot) Vacon had been one of the best known food gatherers and guides that this community, with so many excellent guides, had produced. His life demonstrates some of what I have earlier stated being French speaking Roman Catholic in an English dominated society was like. One winter back in the 30's, Pierrot had been hired to work constructing a dam. Pierrot left the dam to check his trap line and had made more money on the trap line than he had made all winter working on the dam.

Beaver was still the prime catch from the 1930's to the 1960's. Edward still has one of his Grandfather's Beaver tags from 1949 when he had received $40.00 for a prime pelt. This does not mean that he had many Beaver or that the trap line that year made a lot of money. If you had correctly salted away what you needed: your pork, your fish and your beef. If you had cut enough fire wood and had $40.00 hard cash to buy incidentals like flour, sugar, coffee, tea etc., Eulalie said that you could go right through winter in Quinan quite comfortably. Edward explained how some of the village trappers prepared *caches* of food for the winter. They would bring a barrel and some salt with them into the woods around September/October. They would then kill their winter trap line meat, salt it in the barrel, dig a hole in the swamp at a certain spot near their trap line, and bury the barrel. They would dig it up for food while out on the trap line and keep using it until it was gone. The trap line garnished the following animals: bobcats; beaver; otter; fox (mostly red with some silver-grey); and fisher. Lynx are very rare, being endangered in this area. You may hear of one getting caught every 10 – 20 years. Edward, a trapper himself, informed me that a dozen years ago bobcat pelts were worth $1,000.00 apiece. Natural Resources placed a one cat limit on this species even though they are very rare. This author was sitting in a tree stand off the Richmond Road, ten years ago, when a bobcat sauntered in following a rabbit path. The bobcat paused within ten feet from the base of my tree and just sat there for two or three minutes. All of a sudden, he looked up my tree where I was attempting to remain a immobile as possible while I had *company*. He looked right at me for a second time, stood up and calmly resumed his hunt. When asked by a friend why I hadn't shot the bobcat as a trophy, I gave him my two main reasons. Number one, I had a 30-06 Remington rifle and, if I had shot the *Cat*, probably only the lips would have remained. Number two, being single-minded, I was deer hunting, nothing else. You don't shoot what you can't eat!

Edward and George spoke about their Grandfather Pierrot and one of his bear trapping episodes. He used big traps to catch Black Bear and one day he brought a friend, Staley Hatfield, to check one of his bear sites. When they arrived, there was a huge Black Bear in the trap. Although caught, the bear was still quite frisky. Pierrot asked Staley to pass him the rifle but he was told that the gun had been left in the canoe some one and a half miles further on back. Pierrot then told him to give him the axe so that he could finish the job. The bear did not seem to like the idea, lunging at Pierrot, very nearly getting him in the face with his huge paw. Luckily, the trap chain held and Pierrot managed to dodge the blow. A much more prudent Pierrot turned to his friend and said; "Let's go get the gun." Back then, there was a bounty on the bear: $10.00 Federal and $10.00 Provincial. You had to bring in the snout. The bear meat, they ate. Now-a-days, bear trapping has become big business again. You must have a registered bait site and you are issued with a gall bladder tag. That's right, a gall bladder tag. Some Asians grind this up to make an aphrodisiac, a prime specimen bringing up to $1,000.00. Too many people go for the money and waste the meat.

Guiding was a two edged sword. Bringing well-healed Americans or Canadians into the woods to shoot game for the bragging rights and/or the antlers or number of animals that you could shoot in a given period of time could earn a guide good money. But these animals, like the caribou that no longer exist, or the moose that are so few in number in this part of the province that they have no chance of building up their numbers, demonstrate what happens when you are overzealous in the harvesting of a finite resource. All we have left are names like Caribou Plains, once used to describe the sands between Cape Sable Island and the mainland. Moose for home consumption was usually shot around the end of September. They quartered the animal,

*Métis /Acadian food gathers of Quinan after a successful white tail deer hunt in the 1930's.*

placed the meat in the sunlight first, and then wrapped it in wet moss for ten days to cure it, never losing any meat.

White Tail Deer were introduced into Nova Scotia to provide a more prolific species that could keep the hunting tourists coming back to spruce up the economy. The deer too were hunted in volumes that were, at times, unsustainable, and numbers in this part of the province do not compare with other parts of Nova Scotia because the Boston to Yarmouth boats could drop them off right in our back yard where all they wanted to eat or drink could easily be provided with a minimal effort on their part. The guides formed an association, with members from Kemptville, Quinan, and other communities and made motions like not shooting cow moose for a five year hiatus. But motions are not laws, and if your client wanted to take a certain animal, especially if he was just starting to sober up and the hunt was almost over for him, what choice would the guide make if the man who paid the bills was about to go home unhappy.

Like the Tuna Fishing Tournaments that used to take place in Wedgeport, tips made up a sizable part of a guide's income. Only a fool works for nothing right? Both of these groups probably got the *fire and brimstone* speech from their parish priest, Father Joseph Michel Doucet, who served St. Agnes in Quinan the first nine years after his ordination, 29 June1914. A native of Belliveau's Cove, on La Baie Saint Marie, where he was born, 8 May1889, Père Doucet was a strong willed individual who, after leaving Quinan for a six year stint in Plympton, became the cure of St Michel's in Wedgeport till his death in January1953. His faith was so strong that he refused to give the tuna guides permission to work on Sunday, not only to protect them, but also for fear that he would also be condemned by God for letting them go.

*Father (Joseph) Michel Doucet, born Belliveau Cove, Clare, 8 May1889. Ordained priest 29 June1914. Seated here with his alter boys in Saint Michel's Church, Wedgeport. Photo taken circa 1930.*

There are at least four *moose pits* in the Quinan area. I am not certain if they were dug by the Mi'kmag or the Métis/Acadians. This was a successful way of gathering food though not as severe or as successful a method once used by the Métis of the West with their *Buffalo Jumps*. One makes the best use of the tools provided in our natural surrounding. If nothing is wasted – the hunt is just!

One more poignant point I would like to make about our Quinan relatives is how they were exploited as cheap labor during the blueberry harvesting season. In the summer, families would uproot cows, chickens, and themselves to the blueberry picking grounds where they would hire out whole families to the buyers/exporters. Some of the more enterprising families would crate and cellophane blueberries themselves and ship them directly to market. The latter were the exception, not the rule. If they were going picking to far off places like Westmoreland, which was called The *Mountain,* they would have to depart the village with the oxen around 2:00 A.M. in order to arrive there by suppertime. Quite often, they had seasonal camps there, or else they set up tents.

The Tusket River also was once known for its salmon. Locals claim that salmon caught in Quinan could average up to 12 pounds with the largest tipping the scales at a whopping 40 pounds. The Tusket Dam facility combined with the changing Ph factor in the water has caused this river, once a major spawning ground, to die out to the extent that *no* salmon swim upriver today.

In trying to give a sense of the Eastern Woodland Métis Nation Nova Scotia community, I will further, attempt to give example why our community should be taken in the broader sense of encompassing La Hêve, below Kejimkijik National Park and the Tobiatic (of which we make no claim) across to Annapolis County and all points south, with the exception of any provincial parks, rather than just allocating some villages Métis or not. Civilization, through the development of industry, the extension of residential areas, and, in some cases, environmental mismanagement, has created the need to forage further away from the properties we own under the Canadian land ownership system of purchase, survey, register and own.

Food gathering, in the traditional sense, and harvesting of species that either no longer exist in this province, or are on the endangered species list for mainland Nova Scotia, is becoming exceedingly difficult. Our food gathering policy, contained in the last chapter, explains our desire to have a proportional moose draw for the only place that they are still available, Cape Breton Island. Trapping and hunting in someone's back yard with all the pets and/or children that are in danger of being harmed is not practical. Many Métis, including Raymond Muise and the two gentlemen that we are going to track here, Flavien Doucette and André Cottreau, have gone out of their way to assure that they are trapping secluded areas. Their food gathering and trapping carries them away from their home base up into the backwoods of Digby and Annapolis counties. Raymond Muise has provided us with some visual aids while Flavien Doucette has given us a bird's eye view into the mind of a trapper hunter of modern times.

Flavien and André, both former students of mine, are continuing their outdoor activities in the areas that they were brought to by their fathers, the late Laurent Doucette and his buddy, Eddie Cottreau. For almost thirty years these men hunted the territory around New France, the once lumber boom town of the Stehlins, now mostly returned to nature, and the Big Barrio Lake territory. Their interest became their son's interest so it became a yearly event to break free from the village of Wedgeport, take a camper, and beat it up to Barrio early in the hunting season. The boys learned the lay of the land from their fathers. They learned the deer trails, the animal habitat, and how to *navigate* in the woods. It was on one of these trips that these boys, now grown into young men, met a couple of elderly native trappers coming down the Silver River, checking their trap line. After running into the same two trappers a few times, they learned that it was a way for these men to make money and catch food for their family.

A few years went by, the old men were no longer to be seen on the river, and the game: beaver, muskrat, mink, otter, weasel etc. were on the increase again. New beaver dams were popping up everywhere yet there were no trappers to be found around the Barrios. André and Flavien, after discussing the matter, decided to take the training necessary to obtain a fur harvester's permit. Their fathers were impressed because they had done a fair amount of trapping themselves, mostly for rabbits and upland game, in their younger years. The clincher,

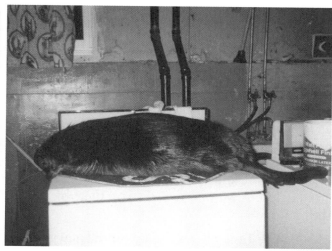

*Raymond Muise and nephew handling freshly caught beaver.*

*Beaver caught in Cape Sable community 9 November 1997.*

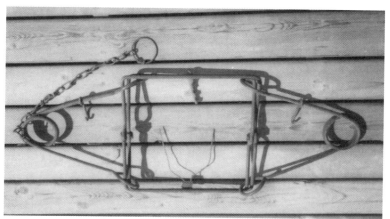

*Conibear trap. Photo by Raymond Muise.*

*Leg-hold traps for beaver. Photo by Raymond Muise.*

of course, was this opening for a source of income and enjoyment in an area where they could deer hunt the dawn and dusk hours and continue the hunt during mid day while checking their trap line. Every morning after the deer hunt, they would get into their 16 foot canoe and paddle up the Silver River towards New France, checking beaver, otter, and mink traps along the river.

Their trap line is about a three hour round trip paddle from the first trap back to the camp. Their initial seasons were only two weeks long, because they all had to return to Wedgeport to get ready for the lobster season. The traps are all removed from the fur habitat. All the animals were brought to Flavien's house where he would skin them and freeze the pelts until sometime in January when the lobster fishery slows down to such an extent that they are lucky to check their pots once a week. After New Years Day, they start trapping again, this time with snares, for bobcats, coyotes, mink and squirrels. The weather may prevent them from checking their trap line every day, yet they keep at it and find it quite rewarding. About twice a week, they go into the shed where André *fleshes out* the fur then together, they put them in wire or wooden frames where they are left to dry for a week or so.

Once dry, they are removed and sent to the local fur handlers for grading sizing and inspection. The furs are all numbered and sent off to different auction houses around the world where furriers purchase them to do their thing – create articles that will sell and allow the process to continue. As rookies, André and Flavien were not too sure that they were doing everything right or that they were maintaining quality like more experienced fur harvesters. Winning five awards for *Top Lot* furs convinced them that they were on the right track. Nothing breeds success like success. After ten years in the business, these Métis/Acadian entrepreneurs have stretched their trap line from New France to the Tusket Islands. They now target different animals in different areas just like the *Big Guys* do. New France and the Barrios provide them with beaver and bobcats while the more saline vicinities around the Tusket Islands offer up their otter, raccoons, and muskrat. They are happy to see more of our young people taking up fur harvesting. Their only regret is that they have as individuals is that they did not begin in earnest a few years earlier. Like all business, you have to spend some money to make some money. You must purchase the proper equipment to harvest (foot hold traps, conibear traps, live cages, submarine cages) and to prepare your furs (proper knives, fleshing beam, stretchers, beaver boards etc). You must further be content with what you are doing and the time it takes to do it. These are the recipes for success.

# Chapter 9.
# Making Our Way into the Twentieth Century

## A. Article 35 of the Canadian Constitution. How it affects us.

The last fifty years of the 20th Century has seen more change in the way man sees things and the way they do things. The Industrial Revolution, instigated in the 19th Century, has been grabbed like a bull by the horns, and those who have it are almost afraid to let go. The two global confrontations of 1914 and 1939 created an urge to take the automobile, the airplane, the vessels of the sea and their many variations to the peak of performance and maneuverability so that one group could save the world from the other group. Let me say, before I continue, that the possibility of living in a Hitler like society still scares the hell out of me. Be that what it may, one of the spin-offs of all military campaigns is that their *improvements and inventions* eventually find their way into the mainstream. Einstein, before he died, wished that he could have taken back the concepts of atomic fusion. Henry Ford and his fellow corporations did their best to supply the war effort but his assembly line production system was taken too much greater extremes than providing two cars in every garage. Fossil fuel emissions are polluting our environment at record levels, the greenhouse effect looking to destabilize Mother Earth's biorhythms.

We not only watch television, but *Big Brother* is looking back at us, tracking our every move through either hidden closed circuit cameras or following the trails left by our bank cards and the other bits of plastic we are told that we need to survive today. Politicians from the main political parties are trying to tell you that they are saving you tax dollars by not adequately dealing with the environment feeling instead that you can't wait to get to the air-conditioned malls where you can spend your tax returns on other taxable items. This in a specially regulated atmosphere, belting out subliminal music and messages that make you happy to be there rather than taking your kids out to enjoy the real world or what's left of it. Big business is cleaning up its act by trying to stay away from being endorsed by young trouble plagued superstars, hoping to pull us in by hiring scandal free older stars like Macdonald's is doing with Paul Newman. I commend their selection but it is too bad that he wants his name tied with fast foods rather than more balanced food choices for a *bulging* North American population.

Do you want a nature fix? The worldwide web can bring you anywhere and give you a much better view if you remain at the computer terminal rather than step outside and see for yourself. Mankind is not satisfied with the good or bad things that are happening on this planet. They prefer to keep us focused on the moon, the stars and the mysteries of the many universes out there. They want to know if we are the most intelligent beings in existence, scared to death to find out that we may be inferior or redundant. People my age remember watching sci-fi movies in the 50's and 60's that showed our superheroes landing their rocket ships on the Moon or Mars, and we brushed it off as comic book stuff. Science proved us wrong but has not proven them all right. The mega funding required servicing the dreams of the very smart give some superpowers a *leg up* on the others but at what a cost. Over half the population of the world does not know how to use a telephone yet alone own one. Some of this stuff and the rationale behind it is mind-boggling. We must buy into ideas that will run the 21ˢᵗ Century but we do not have to become robots to this technology.

Over and over in this book I have stated that it was unwise, for many years, to publicize being of mixed Aboriginal-European blood in this part of the country. For reasons already stated many of us remained silent, tantamount to assimilation, in this part of Canada. A much more radical approach has been taken over the years by our Métis Brothers and Sisters of Ontario and the West. They came after us, establishing Métis communities at a later date as first contact between the Aboriginal and the newcomers tracked west away from the depleted east Many western Métis share the same family names as those who remained in the East. They were raped of their rights and their dignity by consecutive governments, first British, then a Canadian carbon copy of the British system. Great Britain was finding the maintenance of all colonial holding expensive and cumbersome so they decided to cut loose those possessions that would not pose a direct threat to their economy, yet felt British enough to rally to the call of Empire in times of crisis. Welcome Canada- you passed. India failed so they kept their *jewel* for almost another hundred years.

The Canada of 1867 did not look at all like the Canada of today. In fact, the Charlottetown Conference of 1864 had originally been promoted to achieve union of the Maritime Provinces so that the backsliding economies of these smaller political units could unite to form a more viable competitor to Upper and Lower Canada (Ontario & Quebec) and the mercantile New Englanders to the south. John A. Macdonald and cronies got wind of this conference, hood winkled then took over the conference and sold the idea of confederation, an idea that might be seen in a better light today if the Eastern Canadian Provinces had been able to unite first. History records what is - not what might have been. Confederation in an ideal setting guarantees that those Canadians living in Newfoundland have the same expectations of standard of living as those who occupy Ontario. That is what Joey Smallwood promised them in 1949. That is what John A. Macdonald had promised back in 1867. One does not have to look into a financial magazine that analyzes Canadian lifestyles to find out if this is correct or not. Get off the ferry at Port Aux Basques, Newfoundland or cross the border into Windsor, Ontario. They are worlds apart in the same country. .

A basic guarantee of rights and liberties can not change the financial aspirations of Newfoundland to match those of Ontario, but it can level the playing field so that each and every individual in Canada have expectations of same treatment no matter where he lives in Canada. Recognition of the various aboriginal ethnicities in this country can never make up for their past treatment by the governments in power but a serious look was given to this issue in 1981.

At that time, Pierre Trudeau was Prime Minister and Jean Chrétien was Minister of Justice for Canada. They were trying to put together a constitution that would satisfy the needs of *all* Canadians. The President of the Native Council of Canada, an organization founded by the Métis associations in the Prairies and Northwestern Ontario, was Harry W. Daniels. On 30 January 1981, Mr. Daniels received a call from Mr. ChrÈtien informing him that the Special Joint Committee of the House of Commons and the Senate was about to deal with the aboriginal rights provision. This provision was to read: *the aboriginal rights of the aboriginal peoples of Canada are hereby recognized and confirmed.* Mr. Daniels discussed this development with Nunatsiaq's M.P., Peter Ittinuar, insisting that *aboriginal peoples* must include *Indians, Inuit and Métis* so that the terms of reference not lack clarity when dealing with these issues at a later date. Some of the aboriginal leaders were satisfied with the provision as it stood. Minister Chretien heard Harry's concerns, asked him he would go to London to support *patriation* of the Constitution if the provisions were amended. Harry said yes, and then Jean said no, he could not support the Métis insertion to the proposal. A call to Prime Minister Trudeau proved to be the tiebreaker. Pierre said yes and the Conservatives, the N.D.P. and the other concerned powers all agreed. That is how the Section 35 of the Canadian Constitution of 1982 came to be only the second document since the Manitoba Act of 1870 to expressly mention Métis and their rights.[76]

The Native Council of Canada was formed to deal with the Métis of the West and those of Northwestern Ontario. They are interested in the communities and the rights of their Métis members, not ours. That is fair. They have a different history, different grievances, and different expectations for their people than we have in the East. The Manitoba Act 1870 and the Treaty Rights negotiated (dictated) to them dealt with land issues, like the *Script* given to many of them to settle land ownership. Métis and First Nation people were told to go find a 250 acre piece of land that they liked, come back to the surveyor's office, record the land and it was theirs. First Nation concept of land ownership being what it was, most thought that this white man's government was giving them paper for a thing that no one person could own – land. Many a land agent was aware of this and a bottle of whiskey or some other minor item bought perhaps as much as 90% of the script. Some aboriginals were hauled around from one survey office to another to repeat the process. At the end of the day, land ownership was firmly in the hands of the *developers*, and nobody in government (probably on the payroll of the developers) said a word.

Does this mean that there are no Métis outside Ontario coming east? Not at all! I was a registered participant at the 19 November2003 Métis Rights National Forum in Toronto and, not quite an hour into the opening session, when the undercurrent of our non existence was becoming a bit loud, I affirmed my right to belong there as a Métis from Nova Scotia. Tony Belcourt, President of the Métis Nation of Ontario, asked a legal platform up front at the time if there were any Métis in Eastern Canada. The reply came that, according to the Supreme Court Decision in the Powley Case, if they have a site based community that meets the requirements - yes. Let me give you some information picked up on the Department of Indian and Northern Affairs web site which deals with **The Other Métis**. *Several Métis communities came into existence, independently of the Métis Nation, in the eastern part of what we now call Canada, some of them predating the establishment of the Métis Nation. The history of Métis people who are not part of the Métis Nation is not easy to relate. For one thing, their past has not been much studied by historians. If the Métis Nation's story is unfamiliar to most Canadians, the story of the **other** Métis is almost untold. For one thing, their story is made up of several largely unconnected segments; each relating to a different geographic area...Métis peoples in the Maritime Provinces can also trace their communities to early contacts between the Aboriginal populations (Mi'kmaq and Wuastukwiuk, or Maliseet) of the region and French or British newcomers. Rewards were offered by British authorities in the early eighteenth century to British subjects who married Indians...Along with most of the rest of the early Maritime population, Métis people were profoundly affected by the British Expulsion of the Acadians between 1755 and 1763. Métis communities endured or regenerated, however, in parts of what are now Nova Scotia and New Brunswick. One of the earliest recorded uses of the word Métis (Isle Mettise) occurs on a map drawn in 1758 of the area drained by the Saint John River.* [77] I am not here to tell you that the Department of Indian and Northern Affairs published this document because I am not sure. I am certain that it was on their web site in 2003.

At the conclusion of this chapter on **The Other Métis** the following id said: "Even if they were looked upon as a homogeneous collectivity, other Métis would constitute a minority within a minority within a minority: they are a neglected fragment of Canada's Métis population, which is in itself a small and too often overlooked part of the larger Aboriginal minority. Other Métis are not a homogeneous collectivity, of course. They include many discrete communities and groups. Few Canadians are more exposed by their ethnicity to the risks of isolation and alienation than other Métis."[78] There you have it. I wish I could claim to be the author of those words myself, but it is comforting to know that someone else out there is also trying to put our anguish into written language.

On 16 January2004 news hit the wire services indicating that, on the previous day. The federal government had endorsed a *Royal Proclamation* making the tragedy of the Acadian Deportation of 1755 a record of fact. Euclide Chiasson, head of the *Societé Nationale des Acadiens* Better still, the proclamation may eventually be read by the Queen if she accepts the once powerful Sheila Copps' invitation to come to the Maritimes in 2005. Does this mean that they accept the blame and will redress the shame? Keep posted to the wire service for the answer.

# C. The September 19 2003 Supreme Court of Canada Decision Re. Powley and what it Meant for Métis/Acadians

Section 35 of the Constitution Act, 1982 provides:

35 (1) The existing aboriginal and treaty rights of the aboriginal peoples of Canada are hereby recognized and affirmed.

(2) In this Act, "aboriginal peoples of Canada" includes the Indian, Inuit and **Métis** peoples of Canada.

Not all Canadians or our American relatives have followed this legal battle between the Powley's, Steve and Roddy, on the one hand, the Government of Ontario on the other. These members of the Métis Nation of Ontario, living in the community of Sault Ste. Marie, had killed a bull moose on 22 October 1993. They tagged their catch with a tag and a note that stated that they had harvested their meat for winter. Conservation Officers came knocking at their house a week later, charging father and son with hunting moose without a license and unlawful possession of moose. The issue went to court where it was adjudicated in their favor, the decision resting on s.35 of the Constitution of Canada which stated they Powleys had an Aboriginal right to hunt. The Ontario Government appealed but lost again when in January 2000, the Ontario Superior Court of Justice confirmed the earlier decision. The Ontario Government, like good old King Canute of England's Saxon days who had asked the tide not to come in over him (to demonstrate to his people that he could not control everything), took the decision to the Ontario Court of Appeal.

Was it that the Ontario Government thought that it had a righteous case? Perhaps. This *thing* had gotten big with the Métis Nation of Ontario getting help from the Métis National Council because this was to be their test case. A win here would be good for all members. The Ontario Court of Appeal unanimously upheld the Powley's Aboriginal right to hunt as Métis, handing down their decision 23 February 2001. The decision on the Bench was unanimous. Would the Ontario Government throw in the towel? Don't bet on it! There was one more level of justice that they could reach up to, The Supreme Court of Canada. They knew that each time that they went to court, with all of the preparatory pre-trail research and briefs, the Métis would have to dig deeper into their pockets to match government spending in time and quality of defense. The Métis were fortunate enough to be represented by the firm of *Pape and Salter* who were strong on constitutional issues. They felt that they had a winner and could recover court costs when they won. To give the Devil his due, the Ontario Government, along with the Federal Government, had provided the Métis with $300,000.00 for research in 1998. This money financed extensive study at the University of Alberta.

The total court costs for the Powley Court Case began in the fall of 1993 and finally coming to an end two days before fall was to begin in 2003, was in the range of $1,000,000.00. God help any other Métis group that decides to go that route. Bankruptcy can break the soul as well as the pocket book. The Métis National Council, however, thought that the cost was well worth the price when on 19 September 2003 the Supreme Justices of Canada rendered a unanimous decision. They stated: *The development of a more systematic method of identifying Métis rights-holders for the purpose of enforcing hunting regulations is an urgent priority. That said, the difficulty of identifying members of the Métis community must not be exaggerated as a basis for defeating their rights under the Constitution of Canada.*

This author had had the opportunity to read the decision in its entirety and, after some three hours of legal and semi-legal jargonize, I was certain of one thing. The Powley's, as Métis under s.35 Constitution of Canada, had been justified in killing their moose for subsistence. The Court further ruled that the approximately 900 Métis living in the Sault Ste. Marie community also had this right and other food gathering rights similar to the Ojibwa First Nation people living in their vicinity, until the proper paperwork had been completed, establishing their food gathering policy in their own right. The Justices did not take the term community in its greater sense to include the Métis Nation of Ontario nor did it include the territories served by the Métis

National Council. They felt that there were so many Métis communities throughout Canada that it would be foolhardy to give a *carte blanche* to the Métis to *make their pick* to the possible exclusion of others. Instead they set up a basic means to identify Métis rights-holders

The Supreme Court set up three broad factors that could be used to standardize membership requirements throughout Canada and to ensure that there is a verifiable proof in order to substantiate s.35 claims. At the Métis Rights Conference in Toronto, I put out the following proposal on 21 November2003, when the politicians were on the panel, including the Minister for Aboriginal Affairs for the Province of Ontario, home of 1 in 3 Canadians, and a top ranking federal counterpart. The proposal went like this: *"The Federal Government is the top of Canada's political pyramid. In some particular issues, you demand provincial participation. Why not now? Instead of case by case litigation which would undoubtedly be cost prohibitive to many parties, including the governments of Canada – Federal, Provincial, and Territorial, could not a system of research funding, cost shared if necessary, be put into place to identify regional/community Métis groups. This type of research would have impact from all stakeholders and would, in essence, become a springboard to developing a standardized registration system Canada wide. Once the registry's of each Métis community is fully developed there would be an accessible repository in Ottawa.* The Minister from Ontario concurred with me but that is the last I have heard and we are now almost summer 2004. We, of the Eastern Woodland Métis, are not part of the Métis National Council so we must push forward our own agenda. Until registries are developed and accepted, case by case litigation will go on.

Enter the national definition of Métis: ***Métis** means a person who self-identifies as Métis, is distinct from other Aboriginal peoples, is of Historic ancestry, and is accepted by the Métis community.* The Supreme Court Justices broke down the identification process into:

1. Self-identification. The individual must self identify as a member of a Métis community. It is not enough to self-identify as Métis, that identification must have an ongoing connection to an historic community.

2. Ancestral Connection. There is no minimum *blood quantum* requirement, but Métis rights-holders must have some proof of ancestral connection to the historic Métis community whose collective rights they are exercising. The Court said the *ancestral connection* is by birth, adoption or other means. *Other means* of connection to the historic Métis community did not arise with the Powleys and will have to be determined in another case.

3. Community Acceptance. There must be a proof of acceptance by the modern community. Membership in a Métis political organization may be relevant but the membership requirements must also be put into evidence. The evidence must be *objectively verifiable*. That means that there must be documented proof and a fair process for community acceptance.[79]

Before closing this chapter, I would tell you that our Métis Rights Conference, held in the middle of downtown Toronto, was taking place during the fall food gathering season. The Ontario Government's post Powley initiative, at this time, was to instigate a process charging all Ontario Métis out hunting on a case by case basis. The Ministry of Natural Resources was giving these food gatherer's thirty days to have all of the paperwork completed demonstrating that they comply with all the variables set out in the Powley Decision. Tony Belcourt, their leader, told the Ontario Minister that unless the government rescinds this action which had 31 November as the last date, things were going to happen. Belcourt said that there were only 450 Métis Nation of Ontario people exercising their hunting rights in Ontario at this time. Definitely a show of good faith is needed somewhere and the Ontario Government wasn't quite yet ready to play this role. Let us hope that rational minds will work something out in the near future.

# Chapter 10
# Eastern Woodland Métis Nation Nova Scotia

## A. Who We Are and What We Stand For

The totem of the Eastern Woodland Métis Nation Nova Scotia is *le Loup/the Wolf.* The wolf is a social animal much misunderstood by people who do not know him. In order for the species to survive, it must not only have a strong sense of family. This family must stay together, establishing a social order, to guarantee its existence. Lone wolves find it very difficult to survive in the wilderness. If they do not attach themselves to another family, they soon die out.

So it is with our Nation. The Métis of Acadia, an integral part of the early days of this colony, found themselves cut loose from their family ties, along with their First Nation and their Acadian brethren. Hunted like an animal on the verge of extinction, we were allowed to return to our native soil, or what was left of it, in the aftermath of the Acadian Expulsion. The rules laid out for our return were that we swear the Long Oath of Allegiance, that our communities be small, that our lands not be craved by the English or other settlers they brought here, and that we mind our P's and Q's.

Before the Expulsion, we were accepted as part of the Aboriginal or Acadian communities, but set up some of our own, especially in the La Hêve and Cape Sable parts of Acadia. We lived as we willed and where we willed, until we were driven from our homes. Our voice became the lone cry of the wolf for many, many years. We, now, are

*Baylee Morgan Surette, one of our youngest Métis/Acadian members, pointing to the Eastern Woodland Métis totem, the Wolf.*

united families again, and as such we will be heard.

We are not asking for First Nation status. We realize that our ancestors include a large portion of non-aboriginal blood. This does not, however negate our Aboriginal heritage. Many of our Mi'kmaq ancestors perished through the European diseases brought and, at times, spread by the forefathers of those who wanted them gone. They have not all gone but they have been greatly diminished and have been told that the Queen's representatives, in this country, will take care of them as long as they stay on the parcels of land allotted to them and follow the conditions of treaties of shame that keep them tied to these parcels of land like the serfs of old. For many of the Mi'kmaq survivors, they have known nothing else, this *life style* inbred into generation after generation. Some have broken from the mold and gone their own way but it puts them at odds with those who stay.

Our other ancestors, the Métis/Acadian ones, were persecuted, disenfranchised from their quasi-democratic way of life and either removed from this province or forced to live off the hinterland with our Mi'kmaq relatives until cessation of hostilities. The British were more afraid of our close ties with the Indigenous people of this area. They were afraid that we would fight with the Mi'kmaq in a guerilla type warfare rather than stand opposite them in extended rows of musketry, firing away until the less well armed, and less numerous (us), would all die or sue for peace. Sounds like work for a Monty Python's Flying Circus Crack Suicide Squad, not a people hoping to still be around when the madness was gone.

For generations, after France was removed as a player in Canadian affairs, people of French descent were treated as second class citizens by the English victors. Aboriginal descent was seen to be even a lower status as you are well aware of. The Acadian Reserve in this area was not even put in place before 1969, their people trying to survive mostly by living off the land or making baskets and other small items that the whites would buy while looking down at them. Many of our ancestors therefore either denied or would refuse to acknowledge their aboriginal roots.

Thank God, the plight of the Mi'kmaq and the other First Nation peoples has improved over the last fifteen-twenty years, especially as they are gearing up to become much more self-sufficient and may, one day, become their own masters once again. I would reiterate just this once more; we of the Eastern Woodland Métis Nation Nova Scotia do not want to become First Nation Aboriginal with First Nation rights and privileges. We wish to be acknowledged like s.35 Constitution Act 1982 entitles us to be acknowledged. We are not looking for reparations for past injustices. For us, Métis Right recognition by both the Federal and Provincial Governments will give us cultural survival as a Distinct but not separate part of the Canada we all love so much. We wish to develop a clear cohesive collective sense of Métis community that is easily identifiable.

As we stand right now, we have a membership in excess of 3,000 members, mostly living in our community, though some are away and may or may not return some day. The latter Métis I refer to have probably had to go to where the jobs are because there is not a plethora of jobs in this part of the province. However, when they return to the community, their rights are still here for them if they still want to participate in Métis Rights. Another option that may be explored once Métis Communities have been identified across Canada is one of our members being taken in by another Métis community and vice versa. A good example given is Tony Belcourt, originally of Alberta, has risen to become President of the Métis Nation of Ontario. The First Nations have mobility rights; you can move and not lose rights. The Powley Case has not settled this issue.

In our 1979 Declaration of Métis Rights we stated that we are the true Spirit of Canada, and are the source of Canadian Identity. We were assimilated into the Acadian Population or hidden in Indian Communities until 1988 when some of our members looked to revive our Nation. A registry had been opened and faithfully kept though in our region. At one time, there were three Métis organizations: The Yarmouth District Métis; the Kes'pequitik Métis; and our Eastern Woodland Métis. In the fall of 2003, Yarmouth District joined the Eastern Woodland Métis. All members of these groups are out shoots of the same families. The community is the same; the main difference is leadership, a difference that I hope may, at some point in the near future, be resolved.

We have the right to be who we are. The Eastern Woodland Métis Nation Nova Scotia is registered both federally and provincially. We are allied to the Ontario Métis Alliance Inc. "Port McNicoll" with a treaty of mutual respect and rapport, each independent but willing to help out the other. We are also allied with the Métis Women's Circle in Ontario.

Our main office is located at: 1 West Pier 1 Complex Apt. 1A Water Street, Yarmouth Nova Scotia. Our Phone Number is 1-(902)-742- 3304.

The Grand Council Members:

| | |
|---|---|
| Mary Lou Parker- | Nation's Speaker |
| Albert (Tim) Parker- | Chief Senator |
| Gilbert Parker- | Nation's Record Keeper |
| Roland F. Surette- | Chief Captain of the Hunt, Chief Negotiator |
| Adrienne Speck- | Nation's Treasurer |
| Raymond Muise- | Chief Researcher |
| Donald LeBlanc- | Deputy Captain of the Hunt |
| Ernest Samms- | Peace-Keeper |

# B. Eastern Woodland Métis Nation Nova Scotia 2004 Harvesting Policy Revised 01 May2004.

*Whereas* the Métis are one of the Aboriginal peoples of Canada and are recognized as such in *Section 35* of the Constitution Act of Canada;

And *Whereas* harvesting renewable resources ha traditionally been and continues to be integrated to the Métis way of life;

And *Whereas* harvesting renewable resources has traditionally been and continues to be organized by the Captains of the Hunt for the benefit of the Métis community;

And *Whereas* in the Statement of Prime Purpose it is an objective of the Eastern Woodland Métis Nation Nova Scotia to ensure that Métis can continue to exercise their Aboriginal rights;

And *Whereas* the Eastern Woodland Métis Nation Nova Scotia believes that conservation of renewable resources is important and that they have a responsibility to preserve and protect those resources for the benefit of future generations;

And *Whereas* the citizens of the Eastern Woodland Métis Nation Nova Scotia wish to exercise the Métis harvest within a management regime which is self-governed and which recognizes and respects their existing harvesting rights;

*Now Therefore* the Eastern Woodland Métis Nation Nova Scotia declares the following to be the 2004 Harvesting Policy; effective as of the 1st day of September 2004.

1.0     Eligibility

1.1     The issuance of a Métis Harvestor's Permit will be issued under the following guidelines:

(a)     Individuals who are in good standing of the Eastern Woodland Métis Nation Nova Scotia, i.e.: they must have their Métis identification card, the Métis Harvestor's Permit issued to them by the local Captain of the Hunt and any special tags they may have been issued.

(b)     Individuals must be in possession of relevant and valid certificates as required, i.e.; Hunter Safety Certificate, Bow Hunter Certificates, relevant firearms permits.

(c)     Individuals must follow all safety guidelines as set up by the Provincial Department of Natural Resources, i.e.; (i) Hunter Orange must be worn at all times while hunting, exception waterfowl, (ii) relevant survival gear must be on hand, (iii) no hunting on private property unless authorized by the owner in writing.

1.1     This 2004 Eastern Woodland Métis Nation Nova Scotia Harvesting Policy does not create any new Aboriginal Harvesting rights, nor does it limit or expand the existing Aboriginal Harvesting rights of Eastern Woodland Métis Nation Nova Scotia citizens.

1.2     This 2004 Eastern Woodland Métis Nation Nova Scotia Harvesting Policy does not apply to Eastern Woodland Métis Nation Nova Scotia citizens who harvest outside the Province of Nova Scotia. Although we acknowledge that our forbearers signed treaties prior to the division of Nova Scotia in 1784 into the provinces of Nova Scotia and New Brunswick, we do not wish to make this an issue at this time.

1.3     Nothing in this policy precludes an Eastern Woodland Métis Nation Nova Scotia citizen from purchasing a hunting or fishing license from the Department of Fisheries or Natural Resources. However, an individual who does purchase these licenses may not do so to increase higher allotment as designated by this Harvesting Policy.

1.4     This 2004 Eastern Woodland Métis Nation Nova Scotia Harvesting Policy applies only to EWMNNS citizens.

2.0     Objectives

It is an objective of the EWMNNS to encourage conservation practices during the Métis harvest so the species are preserved for future generations. EWMNNS citizens who participate in the Métis Harvest will:

(a)     make best efforts not to destroy or damage fish or wildlife habitat;

(b)     not harvest vulnerable, threatened or endangered species;

(c)     not waste or spoil wildlife or fish; and

(d)     not harvest in fish sanctuaries or in waterfowl sanctuaries.

2.1     It is an objective of the EWMNNS to develop wildlife management practices based on traditional Métis values of cooperation and respect and to encourage EWMNNS citizens who participate in the Métis Harvest will:

(a)     practice safe hunting by taking special care and consideration of other persons, wildlife and property in the area in which they are hunting;

(b)     use firearms safely at all times;

(c)     Take particular care near roads, corridors, forestry or mining operations.

2.1     It is an objective of the Eastern Woodland Métis Nation Nova Scotia to respect the private property rights of landholders. EWMNNS citizens who participate in the Métis Harvest will not harvest on posted, fenced or visibly occupied property unless they have received prior written permission from the landholder.

2.2     In order to better preserve renewable resources for the future, it is an objective of EWMNNS to gather information on all aspects of the Métis Harvest. EWMNNS citizens who participate in the Métis Harvest are encouraged to report to their Captains of the Hunt on their activities, including but not limited to the following:

(a)     area and species harvested;

(b)     the health and number of the species harvested;

(c)     any encounters with Ministry of Natural Resources or Department of Fisheries and Oceans compliance officers;

(d)     any problems or observations that may be relevant to the species, habitat or Métis harvesters; and

(e)     Environmental concerns which may affect the species, habitat or Métis harvesters.

2.1     Captains of the Hunt are appointed to enable the effective management of the Métis Harvest. The EWMNNS believes that community consultation is a key element of this effective management regime. Captains of the Hunt shall consult with the EWMNNS communities in their region before making recommendations which may in any manner limit the Métis Harvest.

2.2     All other parts of this policy are to be interpreted consistently with the objectives in this part.

3.0     Métis Harvest

3.1     A EWMNNS citizen who is authorized by the EWMNNS and issued a EWMNNS Harvester's Certificate by a Captain of the Hunt may participate in the Métis Harvest in accordance with this policy.

3.2     The Métis Harvest shall be in accordance with the allotments designated in Sections 5.0, 6.0, 7.0 and 8.0 of this Harvesting Policy

3.3     A Captain of the Hunt may recommend to the Chief Captain of the Hunt that:

(a)     The season for any species, be abridged or curtailed in his or her region for conservation or safety reasons:

(b)     The season be extended in his or her region for deer;

(c)     Allocations or limitations on the Métis Harvest be made for conservation reasons: e.g. cease pending hunts or fishing of endangered species like salmon (non land-locked).

3.4     A EWMNNS Citizen may apply to a Captain of the Hunt for an EWMNNS Harvesters Certificate which shall be valid for one year Such applicants shall provide a Captain of the Hunt with demonstrated proof of the following:

(a)     If the applicant intends to use firearms in the Métis Harvest, he or she must demonstrate sufficient knowledge of the firearms safety or a completion of a firearms safety course; and

(b)     That he or she is ordinarily a resident and intends to participate in the Métis Harvest in his or her traditional territory which is in the Province of Nova Scotia.; or

(c)     That a direct ancestor was a beneficiary of a Nova Scotian treaty and that he or she is ordinarily resident and intends to participate in the Métis harvest in that treaty area.

3.5     For purposes of participation in the Métis Harvest, a Captain of the Hunt may issue a EWMNNS Certificate which shall be considered proof that the holder has been verified by the EWMNNS Registrar as having provided sufficient documentation to support a claim to an Aboriginal or treaty right to harvest.

3.6     Captains of the Hunt shall advise EWMNSS Citizens to carry their EWMNSS Citizenship Card when participating in the Métis Harvest and to show it to Ministry of Natural Resources (MNR) compliance officers.

3.7     EWMNNS Citizens who hold a EWMNNS Harvesters Certificate agree to harvest in accordance with the objectives in Section 2 of this policy.

3.8     EWMNNS Harvesters Certificate holders may harvest with persons who have lawfully obtained licenses and tags issued by MNR or by a First Nation.

3.9     Harvesting which is carried out in violation of this policy may result in withdrawal of the EWMNNS Harvesters Certificate or a refusal by their Chief Captain of the Hunt to renew the EWMNNS Harvesters Certificate.

4.0    Captain of the Hunt

4.1    The Grand Council of the EWMNNS shall appoint the Chief Captain of the Hunt. He or she shall have the overall management of the Métis Harvest within the Province of Nova Scotia and the coordination of the regional Captains of the Hunt.

4.2    The Captain of the Hunt shall certify each regional Captain of the Hunt as appointed by their Circle. He or she shall be responsible to implement this policy in accordance with the objectives laid out in Article 2.

4.3    Captains of the Hunt shall determine the appropriate management of the Métis Harvest and shall evaluate its progress on an ongoing basis and no less that twice a year shall report to the Chief Captain of the Hunt.

4.4    Pursuant to Article 2.4, Captains of the Hunt shall make best efforts to collect and disseminate harvest information obtained from EWMNNS Citizens who are participating in the Métis Harvest.

4.5    Captains of the Hunt may, after consultation with the Chief Captain of the Hunt, withdraw EWMNNS Certificates on written notice with reasons to the certificate holder. Persons whose EWMNNS Harvesters Certificates have been withdrawn may appeal such decision to the Chief Captain of the Hunt.

4.6    Despite the seasonal limitations in Article 3.2, Captains of the Hunt may designate a person or persons to harvest for the benefit of the EWMNNS Citizens in a particular Métis Community. The proceeds of such harvest may be used for, among other things, sharing, social or ceremonial purposes.

5.0    Allotments for the Eastern Woodland Métis Nation Nova Scotia.

Each Métis Harvester, having the proper identification card, Harvesters Certificate from his or her Captain of the Hunt; and special tags (if required) may harvest the following species as outlined;

5.1 Deer – A EWMNNS member in good standing with the proper certificates and tags may harvest a maximum of two deer per season. In order to maintain this renewable resource, the gatherer must harvest either two male deer (bucks) or one male and one female (doe). A household may not have more than four deer taken within one hunting season which runs from mid September to December 31.

5.2 Moose – A EWMNNS member in good standing with the proper certificates will be eligible to enter their name in a lottery. Only one person per household will be allowed to enter this lottery during any given year. The successful participant will be issued a tag and a report card that is to be filled in after (a) the successful completion of a hunt or (b) December 31 of this given year. A person who has successfully harvested a moose will be ineligible to submit their name in the draw for the next two years. A Métis who is unable to fill in his or her tag may request that another member of the EWMNNS, who has the proper requirements, fill in their tag for them.

5.3 Black Bear - A EWMNNS member in good standing who has the proper certificates and a registered bait site may request permission from the Captain of the Hunt to exercise this right. The bear must be harvested by using a firearm or a bow. Poisoning or setting up a blind trap, where there is a gun rigged to be automatically triggered when the bear takes the bait, is prohibited.

5.4 Fur Bearing Animals – A EWMNNS member in good standing will be allowed to receive a trapping certificate and report card from the Captain of the Hunt. He or she must remain within the quota and guidelines set up by the Province of Nova Scotia and the Government of Canada.

5.5 Small Game – Members of the EWMNNS are allowed to gather for personal consumption any, non endangered animal of the land or fish of the seas that are not further regulated below, on a year round basis.

(a) Fowl – Pheasant, Partridge, Grouse etc. a maximum of fifteen in your possession at any one time.

(b) Migrating Birds – a maximum of ten migrating birds that are not endangered at any one time.

(c) Maximum Fowl and/or Migrating Birds in a *household* shall not exceed 20.

5.6 Fresh Water Fish – All Provincial Government guidelines will be respected with the exception of *Trout* of which a EWMNNS member will be allowed to possess a maximum of ten (10) on any given day.

6.0 Saltwater Fish

Members of the Eastern Woodland Métis Nation Nova Scotia will be allowed to follow these guidelines with regards to harvesting the oceans and the river estuaries of Nova Scotia. Once again it is clearly stated that this is for non commercial purposes. All Métis Harvesters shall follow and respect the zones and areas for harvesting as set by the Provincial Department of Natural Resources and the Federal Department of Fisheries and Oceans. A EWMNNS member who exceeds the following quotas will place himself or herself beyond the protection of this 2004 Harvesting Policy. They will have to take their own chances in a court of law. A harvester found guilty of excess harvesting beyond the limits found in this Policy will also face sanctions by the Eastern Woodland Métis Nova Scotia.

6.1 A member of the EWMNNS in good standing will be allowed to catch up to twenty (20) ground fish of any species per day, with the exception of *Halibut*, which has a limit of one (1).

6.2 Individuals from the EWMNNS will be allowed to dip five (5) dozen Smelts per day. Hand lines are also permitted.

6.3 Members will be allowed to harvest an unlimited amount of Mackerel, Herring and/ or Gasperaux for food or ceremonial purposes.

6.4 Salmon and other endangered species - Members of the EWMNNS will respect the guidelines laid out by the Department of Fisheries and Oceans. However, the EWMNNS reserve the right to renegotiate areas and totals as circumstances permit.

6.5 EWMNNS members are allowed to harvest Shark and any other non endangered non commercial fish from the water systems surrounding Nova Scotia.

7.0 Crustaceans

7.1 EWMNNS individuals are entitled to harvest a maximum of a two (2) gallon bucket of clams for home consumption.

7.2 EWMNNS members may harvest 100 Cohogs, Bar Clams or Scallops, to feed their families. The limits are the same for traditional gatherers or divers.

7.3 Any species not specifically mentioned above falls under the same guidelines as its nearest crustacean relative unless not regulated at all.

7.4 EWMNNS members who go over the prescribed limits are open to prosecution by the non native laws of Canada as well as sanctions by the EWMNNS..

7.5 Lobster – Each member in good standing of the EWMNNS shall be allowed to harvest Lobster off the shores of Nova Scotia. The methods used will be one trap (requires EWMNNS tag) or diving (requires EWMNNS Certificate). The Lobster must be harvested during the same season as the commercial fishery but not for commercial reasons. Harvesters will be allowed a twenty (20) pound limit of legal sized Lobster in the shell on any given day. The household possession limit is not to exceed fifty (50) pounds in the shell, at any given time. Harvesting undersized Lobster, or over fishing these limits, leave you accountable to the non native laws and automatically suspends your membership and Métis rights until clarified in a court of law.

8.0 The Eastern Woodland Métis Nation of Nova Scotia maintains the right to renegotiate all harvesting rights to any of the pre-negotiated species as well as any species of animal or fish not covered in this Policy.

Policy first presented to N.S. Ministry of Natural Resources and Department of Fisheries and Oceans, Canada, 21 June2001. Revised by Roland F. Surette, Chief Captain of the Hunt EWMNNS, 1 April2004

The document is **not in force yet** and will not be in force until we have come to an agreement with the Province of Nova Scotia, establishing our Métis Rights. The main rationale behind hand delivering copies of our Food Gathering Policy on 21 June2001 was that, in many cases, when you start at the top it may go no further than the top. The people in the trenches, the actual men and women who deal with the enforcement of policies such as this one, very seldom have a chance to give their own input. It is also their duty to pass this kind of document up the chain and, once I had officials in both offices sign for the policy, I knew the proper protocols would be adhered to.

On 14 September2001, I received a response from the Department of Fisheries and Oceans (Photocopy of original document in book). You can look over this letter where you will find, in the second paragraph, that DFO and Native Council of Nova Scotia (NCNS) had negotiated an "agreement on fisheries access for the off-reserve, non-status and *Métis* people in Nova Scotia". The third paragraph described DFO's *expectation* that the NCNS "administer access to the fishery in a fair and just way for all the people they represent". This letter originated in Ottawa, where I was told that their legal department began looking at our policy within two days of receiving it. It was signed by Alan J. Clarke A/Area Director DFO for South West Nova Scotia in my presence when I accepted his right to sign on behalf of DFO.

The letter shows that they expected we would realize our plans for the fall fishing season but the First Nation groups of this province, fearful that somehow we would try to cut into their cash cow, fought our inclusion. We did not *go to war* on this issue. All of our members have been repeatedly told by me, or my representatives, until they heard from me personally or saw me declaring our Food Gathering Policy in effect in the media; they were to abstain from any Métis activity that might place us in conflict with the laws of this land. It is with great pride that I can say that, to date, they have adhered to this directive.

The 19 September2003 Powley Supreme Court ruling has changed the playing field. Its contention, confirming the Canadian Constitution Act 1982, that *Métis* are Aboriginal in their own right, means that we no longer require sanctioning from our First Nation brethren. In the letter, DFO recognized that there are Métis in Nova Scotia and that these Métis have rights. We are Métis of Acadia and we will be counted.

C. Closing Remarks and a Peek at the Future.

The 60's and 70's bred the fight for what's right generation. I am a part of that generation. Supreme sacrifices had been made by previous generations to insure not only our freedoms, but also that we should stand tall and not let the freedoms of others be denied. Strange? We had asked people from all walks of life to participate yet those who came from reserves, even if they were decorated vets, were denied access to their local Royal Canadian Legion if liquor/beer was being sold. This was just maintaining a false belief established in the 17th and 18th centuries that told us liquor and Indians do not mix. The European traders who preached that on Sundays sold brandy and whiskey to rip off the Indians on Monday. I am not stating that first contact with alcohol is not a dangerous thing. It was bad back then and it is bad now. First Nation society was perhaps not geared for intoxicants of this nature in the beginning. The same holds true for European society when they first began using the *strong stuff*.

By the time that aboriginal society got used to alcohol and other imported vices their society was in turmoil. They were the *Have Nots* being told what they were missing by the *Haves*. These *Haves* soon began taking from the Native peoples – first their dignity, then their property, then their land. You place any population in this type of dead end situation, get them used to drowning their sorrows as long as they don't bother you and your expectations will become reality. Therefore what society wants, society gets. We of mixed heritage decided to bypass this denigration by stating that we were Acadian and left it at that. Being of French Roman Catholic descent in the Post Deportation years was bad enough without heaping more grief on ourselves in an English world. Money talks and the rest of us walk. We knew who ruled the roost and we knew that change would be slow.

| Fisheries and Oceans | Pêches et Océans |

215 Main Street
Yarmouth, Nova Scotia
B5A 1C6

Your file     Votre référence

Our file     Notre référence

September 14, 2001

Roland Surette
Captain of the Hunt
Métis Nation of Nova Scotia
RR # 2 South Ohio
Yarmouth County, NS
B0W 3E0

## RE:  Métis Nation of Nova Scotia 2001 Harvesting Policy

Dear Mr. Surette:

We are in receipt of your 2001 Harvesting Policy.  As you know, the Department of Fisheries and Oceans has been providing Aboriginal communities with access to food, social and ceremonial fisheries since 1992.  In addition, we have been providing Aboriginal communities access to commercial fisheries since 1994.

The Department of Fisheries and Oceans (DFO) enters into fishing arrangements with First Nations.  However, DFO and the Native Council of Nova Scotia (NCNS) have negotiated an agreement on fisheries access for the off-reserve, non-status and Métis people in Nova Scotia.

It is certainly DFO's expectation that the NCNS would administer access to the fishery in a fair and just way for all the people they represent.  I would encourage you to work with the Native Council of Nova Scotia in an effort to realize your plans for the fall fishing season.

Yours truly,

Alan J. Clarke
A/Area Director, SWNS

The social safety net was non existent in the 18th, 19th, and the first half of the 20th Centuries. Elders depended upon family members in their declining years. Sometimes no matter how many children you had, none survived to set up a household safety net. Infertile couples would adopt children from large families and the actual biological components of a person could be lost in the shuffle. This is why at times acceptance into the Métis/Acadian community was as close as you could get to being rock certain about your genes. Our people took care of themselves. With so many men going to sea because the new lands could not provide the entire wherewithal to raise a family, many perished. The women could not forever morn these tragedies; they would get on with their lives, remarry, more than once if the situation demanded it. If families were burnt out or struck by some affliction, villagers would pitch in to put these unfortunates back on their feet. We became insular of necessity but that was not always a bad thing. Our language (French), our religion and our *joie de vivre*, to celebrate the good times and remember the bad, survived mainly because of it.

The English expected long term assimilation and, in many ways, they were right. Our lands, our waters, and our lifestyle were taken from us but many came back, regrouped, resettled, learned to suppress our anger and our identity. As Acadians our resettlement was

*Author and his son, Morgan, outside a teepee at Fort Edmonton, Alberta, July1986.*

allowed initially as long as we did not settle any one place in large numbers that could mount any threat to the new government and as long as we did not ask for our old homesteads to be returned, especially our lands that had been given to entice the Planters from New England or disbanded soldiers who had been so rewarded.

One of our most flamboyant Prime Ministers, whose ancestors had walked our walk, decided to do something about rooting out inequality on the political platform in the 1980's. Pierre Elliot Trudeau had also witnessed the radically different tact taken by our neighbors to the South. The racial riots, the wars of domination in the Far East, the protest movement that took hold because big brother was trying to make a little brother into a smaller version of himself. All of these events made Prime Minister Trudeau realize that a constitutionally guaranteed Bill of Rights must be in place with all the protocols to protect it. I believe his own experience with the F.L.Q. and the institution of Martial Law in this country had a sobering effect as well.

The Canadian Constitution Act 1882 recognizes Métis Rights. We are who we are due to an act of God that placed our ancestors in each others arms over the generations. Like the other various Métis communities across Canada, we are the same but different. Those of European ancestry who controlled our world in the past would deny our existence today as their forebearers did in yesteryear. Our brethren, the Mi'kmag People, once a numerous and powerful nation, fear our numbers might cut their stipends from the government of today. It is very difficult to get provinces to agree on what national standards are. How different is it to assume that

# RESOLUTION

**MOVED BY:** Wayne Gaudet, MLA
Clare

Mr. Speaker, I hereby give notice that on a future day I shall move the adoption of the following resolution:

**WHEREAS** the Metis Nation has a long history and deep roots here, in the Maritime Provinces; and

**WHEREAS** the Eastern Woodlands Metis Nation Nova Scotia represents and responds to the political, cultural, social and economic needs and interests of Metis Aboriginal people in this Province;   and

**WHEREAS** the Eastern Woodlands Metis Nation has identified over 3000 Metis people in Nova Scotia and they wish to be officially recognized in this Province.

**THEREFORE BE IT RESOLVED** that the members of this House call on the Government to meet with representatives of this group to better understand the history of the Metis people in this Region, and that the government consider giving an appropriate form of Provincial recognition to the Eastern Woodlands Metis Nation of Nova Scotia.

Mr. Speaker I ask for waiver of notice and passage without debate.

Métis groups across Canada may have different standards? The western Métis developed around the buffalo and the prairies; the northern Métis developed around the polar bear, the seal and the ice fields; the eastern Métis developed around the beaver, the moose, and the sea. Our communities were developed at different times and under different situations therefore expectations are different.

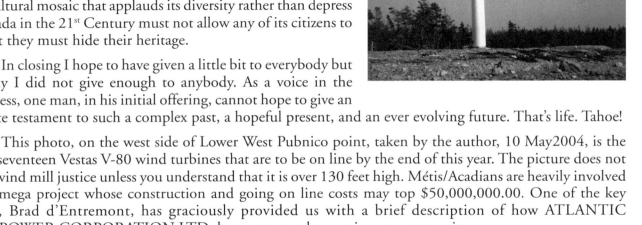

We were here, we were silenced, but we are here today and we wish to be silenced no more. All we ask is that our circle of life be acknowledged to be complete. Will there be issues to be resolved – yes. Can they be resolved without gutting the public purse and placing the management of our community in jeopardy – yes. Education did not come easily to many generations of our Métis/Acadian predecessors yet it did come thanks to the will to survive in a sometimes hostile environment and the push given to us by people like Father Jean Mande Sigogne. Combine this with the coming of age of Canadian citizenry at large that now form a multicultural mosaic that applauds its diversity rather than depress it. Canada in the 21st Century must not allow any of its citizens to feel that they must hide their heritage.

In closing I hope to have given a little bit to everybody but probably I did not give enough to anybody. As a voice in the wilderness, one man, in his initial offering, cannot hope to give an adequate testament to such a complex past, a hopeful present, and an ever evolving future. That's life. Tahoe!

This photo, on the west side of Lower West Pubnico point, taken by the author, 10 May2004, is the first of seventeen Vestas V-80 wind turbines that are to be on line by the end of this year. The picture does not do the wind mill justice unless you understand that it is over 130 feet high. Métis/Acadians are heavily involved in this mega project whose construction and going on line costs may top $50,000,000.00. One of the key players, Brad d'Entremont, has graciously provided us with a brief description of how ATLANTIC WINDPOWER CORPORATION LTD. has come to take root in our community.

"The idea of producing electricity with wind energy began as a topic of conversation between Brad d'Entremont, Allister d'Entremont and Joerg Losse about three years ago. Joerg had been involved in developing wind farms in his native Germany over several years and still owned four windmills. Brad and Allister felt the potential for harnessing a farmable amount of wind on Pubnico point was worth investigating and began measuring the wind speed and direction using a 30m met mast at the site. Shortly thereafter, Nova Scotia Power put out a request for proposals for private companies to develop a wind farm capable of producing 100GWH of energy per year. At that time a fourth partner, Charles Demond, joined the group as Vice-President of Business Development.

Over the next three years Brad and Allister worked at acquiring land, having it surveyed, collecting wind data, acquiring of necessary permits and educating the community and municipal officials on the pro's and con's of wind farms. Joerg and Charles focused on the requirements of Nova Scotia Power, choosing the right turbine manufacturer and the legal/financial aspects of the project.

Our company, Atlantic Wind Power Corporation Ltd. was awarded the contract to up to seventeen Vestas V-80 wind turbines in two phases, two wind mills by May 2004 and the remaining fifteen by the end of 2004."

Brad d'Entremont, 15 May2004

# Notes

1 *Newfoundland Lifestyle 2000 Commemorative Issue.* St. Johns, Newfoundland. (2000) pp. 16 – 18

2 *The Argus.* Volume 14.No. 2. Summer, (2002) Tusket, Nova Scotia. p. 35

3 Wallace K. Ferguson, Geoffrey Brunn, *A Survey of European Civilization*, Third Edition. Houghton Mifflin Co., Boston, U.S.A. p. 368

4. Don Gilmor, Pierre Turgeon. *Canada – A People's History.* Volume 1. C.B.C. Production. McClelland and Stewart Ltd., Toronto, Ontario. (2000)
p. 29

5. Wallace K. Ferguson, Geoffrey Brunn, *A Survey of European Civilization*...p. 374

6. Ibid., p. 377

7. Sally Ross, Alphonse Deveau, *The Acadians of Nova Scotia Past and Present.* Nimbus Publishing Ltd. Halifax, Nova Scotia. (1992) p. 20

8. Edith Firoozi, Ira N. Klien. *The Universal History of the World.* Vol. IX. Golden Press Inc. New York, U.S.A. (1996) p. 721

9. Ibid., Page 721.

10. Ann McGovern. *If You Sailed the Mayflower.* Scholastic Book Services. New York, U.S.A. (1969) p.54

11. Ibid., p. 76.

12. Daniel Paul. *We Were Not the Savages.* Fernwood Publishing, Halifax, Nova Scotia (2000) p. 42

13. Don Gilmor, Pierre Turgeon, *Canada – A Peoples History.* Page 20

14. Daniel Paul, *We Were Not the Savages.* p. 10

15. Ibid., p. 12

16. Ibid., Page 26

17. *The Illustrated Library of the World and its Peoples.* Vol. 2. Greystone Press, New York, U.S.A. (1967). p. 264

18 Ibid. P. 264

19. Charles D. Mahaffie Jr. *A Land of Discord Always.* Nimbus Publications, Halifax, Nova Scotia. (1995) p.18

20. Daniel Paul, *We Were Not the Savages.* p. 23

21. Halifax Chronicle Herald, Section B. 09 March 2004. Article by Beverly Ware – "Champlain's Landing Site Recognized."

22. Daniel Paul, *We Were Not the Savages.* p. 16

23. Ibid. p. 23

24. Ibid. p. 28

25. Alpsonse Deveau. *Two Beginnings – A Brief Acadian History.* Lescarbot Publications. Yarmouth, Nova Scotia. (1980) p. 70

26. G.P.Gould, A.Semple. *Our Land the Maritimes.* Saint Anne's Point Press. Fredericton, New Brunswick. (1980) p. 14

27. Henri-Dominique Paratte. *Acadians.* 2nd Edition. Nimbus Publishing Ltd., Halifax, Nova Scotia. (1998) p. 28

28. R.V. Unstead. *Struggle for Power 1485-1689.* Vol. IV. Macdonald Educational Ltd. Hollywell House, London, England. (1972) p. 59

29. Don Gilmor, Pierre Turgeon. *Canada-A People's History.* p. 103

30. Henri-Dominique Paratte, Acadians 2nd Edition... p. 30

31. Lafayette Daily Advertiser, Supplement, 29 September 1994. Lafayette, Louisiana, U.S.A. Article by Jim Bradshaw. *Remembering Our Acadian Heritage.* p. 2

32. Sally Ross, Alphonse Deveau. *The Acadians of Nova Scotia.* p. 7

33. Ibid. p. 10.

34. Ibid. p. 11.

35. Lafayette Daily Advertiser, Supplement, 29 September1994. p. 8

36. Ibid. p. 9.

37. Ibid. p. 11.

38. Sally Ross, Alphonse Deveau. *The Acadians of Nova Scotia.* p. 15

39. Alphonse Deveau. *Two Beginnings.* p. 32

40. Ibid., p. 33.

41. Charles D. Mahaffie Jr. *A Land of Discord Always...* p. 78

42. Ibid. pp. 83-84

43. Stephen White.
*Dictionnaire Genealogique des Familles Acadiens.* Centre d'Etudes Acadiennes, Université de Moncton. Moncton, Nouveau Brunswick. (1999) p. 7

44 Ibid. p. 6

45. Alphonse Deveau.
*Two Beginnings.* p. 32

46. Steven White. English supplement to the *Dictionnaire Genealogique des Familles Acadiennes.* Centre d'Etudes Acadiennes, Université de Moncton. Moncton, New Brunswick. (2000) p. 105

47. Nicolas Denys. *Description geographique des costes de l'Amerique Septentrionelle.* Paris, France. (1672) pp. 123-124

48. Steven White. English Supplement... p. 106

49. Charles D. Mahaffie Jr. *A Land of Discord Always.* pps. 83-84

50. Lafayette Daily Advertiser, Supplement, 29 September1994. p. 15

51. Stephen White. English Supplement... pp. 112-113

52. Clarence J. d'Entremont *Priest. Histoire de Cap-Sable De l'An Mil Au Traite de Paris (1763). Volume 3.* Hébert Publications, Eunice, Louisiana 70535. (1981) pp1418-1419

53. Ibid. pp.1424-1425

54. Stephen White. English Supplement ...p158

55. Daniel Paul. *We Were Not the Savages...* p78

56. Ibid...pp79-80

57. Comite de genealogie Wedgeport. *Les Familles du Bas-de-Tousquet (Wedgeport) 1767 a 1900.* Les Editions Lescarbot, Wedgeport, Nouvelle-Ecosse. B0W 3P0 (1992) pp 339 and 334

58. Ibid...p 338

59. Jacques Levron. *History of France – Concise History of Great Nations* General Editor, Otto Zierer Leon Amiel Publisher, New York, N. Y. 10036 (1977) p71

60. Ibid...p67

61. Sally Ross Alphonse Deveau. *The Acadians...*p56

62. Daniel Paul. *We Were Not the Savages...*p95

63. Jacques Levron. *History of France...*pp71-72

64. Charles D. Mahaffie Jr. *A Land of Discord...*p191

65. Henri Dominique Paratte. *Acadians...*pp47-48

66. J. Alphonse Deveau. *Two Beginnings...*p85

67. Charles Mahaffie Jr. *A Land of Discord...*p241

68. J. Alphonse Deveau. *Two Beginnings...*pp88-89

69. Daniel Paul. *We Were Not the Savages...*p116

70. Rev. J.R. Campbell. *A History of the County of Yarmouth, Nova Scotia*
Originally published by J. A. McMillan Saint John N.B. 1876 Copyright (1997) Argyle Municipality Historical & Genealogical Society p28

71. Henri Dominique Paratte. *Acadians* ... p43

72. Lafayette Daily Advertiser, Supplement, 29 September1994...p38

73. Ibid...p37

74. J. Alphonse Deveau. Two Beginnings... p116

75. Frank Pothier. *Acadians at Home1765* Self Publicized Yarmouth N.S. 1957. Parts of benefits to Canadian Cancer Society p10

76. Tony Belcourt, President of Métis Nation of Ontario *Presentation at National Forum – The Supreme Court of Canada Recognizes Métis Rights* Toronto 20 November2003 pp6/7

77. *Perspectives and Realities* Vol. 4 Chapter 5 Métis Perspectives Section 3 *The Other Métis* pp1/2

78. Ibid p. 5

79. Fulfilling Canada's Promise – Metis Rights. Recognized and Assumed. R. V. Powley A Case Summary Nov. 2003 Metis National Council Ottawa p. 6

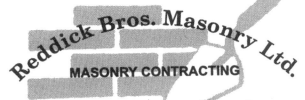

## ADCL
## Commercial Rental Space
Phone: 902-645-2451
Meteghan River, Digby Co.,
Nova Scotia B0W 2L0

**Chris d'Entremont**
MLA/Député, Argyle

Tel/tél: 902-648-2020
Fax/téléc: 902-648-2001
info@chrisdentremont.com
www.chrisdentremont.com

NOVA SCOTIA
NOUVELLE-ÉCOSSE

---

## Acadian Bowling Lanes

Tel: (902) 769-2217
Little Brook
Nova Scotia B0W 1Z0

## J.N.J. Fisheries Limited

124 North Ohio Road
South Ohio
Nova Scotia B0W 3E0

---

## Le Pain de Chez Nous Ltée.

Tel: (902) 769-2419
PO Box 40, Saulnierville
Nova Scotia B0W 2Z0

## Wedgeport Fuels Limited

R.R. 1, Box 4080
Tel: (902) 663-2244
Arcadia
Nova Scotia B0W 1B0

---

## Marco's Grill & Pasta House

Tel: (902) 648-0253
237 Gavel Road, R.R. 3
Tusket, Nova Scotia B0W 3M0

## Rakell Fisheries Limited

Tel: (902) 663-2393
Wedgeport
Nova Scotia B0W 3P0

---

## Taverne Acadienne Ltd. et
## Restaurant Evangeline
ice depuis Juillet 15, 1963
Tel: (902) 645-3660
Meteghan River
Nova Scotia B0W 2L0

## Jake's
## Diner & Pizzeria

Fast Free Delivery In Town
*—Out of Town Delivery Available*
"Quality, Service, Variety, Low Prices"

742-8882 • 322 Main St. • Yarmouth, N.S.